Charting Polar Seas

The life, careers and interests of Adam Kerr

Chart-maker, sailor and fisherman

ISBN: 978-1-326-57316-4

Typesetting and cover design by Oxford Literary Consultancy

Glyn,

With Best Wishes from

Adam

25 May 2016

Dedicated to my sons, Andrew and Timothy

CONTENTS

ILLUSTRATIONS

Acknowledgements

I have used many pictures in this book. Most of them are from private collections. Where other photos have been used I have attributed them to the photographer. In a few cases there is no information about the source of the photograph.

A TASTE OF THE SEA

Early Days

The framework of a good story and particularly an autobiography is often hardship. However this was not my case. I have moved through life without having had to experience any great traumas, such as deaths, serious illnesses or accidents. My life story therefore has been based mainly on fortuitous circumstances and perhaps luck. I have in fact seen very few dead bodies, apart from those of my maternal grandfather and my mother. To a great extent although I have lived through one World War and numerous lesser disputes, such as the Korean War or the more recent battles in the Middle East, I have never been expected to take up arms. By contrast, my father served in two World Wars, participated in the D-Day invasion and was never wounded in any way. So this story is of a life that moved forward through a series of events and actions that were largely unplanned apart from my earlier school years. At the back of it must have been a strong wish to succeed in whatever I did and perhaps to be happy. I think my parents had a large part to play in these ambitions, although their influence was subtle. I have always felt how important it is to have a united family behind the 'parenting' of offspring. I sometimes dwell on the importance of genealogy and wonder just how much it influences our lives. Certainly in my case, as you will read, the reasons why I followed a seagoing career and had a strong interest and some limited ability in the arts must surely be due to the influence of my parents. However, was it just interest or was the sea in my blood? Or an artistic ability hidden in my veins? Certainly I can recognise that I am the grandson of a famous artist and my mother was a capable and talented painter and that both my sons have also shown that they have a significant artistic ability. They have only shown a limited interest in sailing, but a determined interest and ability in surfing, although when actually put to the task of going to sea in boats, they are also perfectly capable in that pursuit.

I was born in Chelsea, London in 1933. This is somewhat to my chagrin because I would liked to have a firm allegiance to either Cornwall or Scotland by being born in one of those places but my parents must have decided that they be in London to deliver me into this World.

My first introduction to the sea came early in my life. My father, Jimmy Kerr, was a writer, who had travelled the Globe as a sailor, roustabout and hobo. I came into this world when he was trying hard to establish a reputation as an author. When I was two my father presented his publishers with the idea that they would advance him the cash to acquire a boat, in which he would make a trip up the West Coast of Scotland and write a book about the venture. All this came to pass and his book Cruising in Scotland (Collins 1938), which relates the story. Briefly, he persuaded his publishers to advance him £25 with which he bought a 29 foot ship's lifeboat for £9. He moved the boat to the River

Cart, which runs through Paisley in Scotland and set about converting this old hull into a motor-sailer.

Figure 1 *Migrant* in a Scottish Loch. Private collection.

The story of this conversion is related in the book and is a tale on its own. Scrounging materials from the local shipyards and aided by the rather spasmodic help of an unreliable carpenter Chippy, he made a fine little cruising boat. My father originated from Paisley, so he was in familiar territory and as a family we stayed near the building site. The River Cart enters the Clyde River and across the Clyde was the famous John Brown's Shipyard where the *Queen Mary* was being built at that time. The family scrap book shows my father rowing some people across the Clyde in our dinghy. It is not clear how long the conversion took to complete but it was considerably lengthened by the frequent absence of Chippy, who had a good thirst for alcohol. Eventually the boat was ready and my mother and grandparents boarded. How our family fitted into a 29 foot boat is not clear. Especially as there was also a dog and at times a nanny! This was my first taste of the sea and I was three when the little boat finally motored down the Clyde.

Figure 2 SJ Lamorna Birch, *Migrant* in Loch Riddon, watercolour.

That first season was spent exploring the many lochs and inlets that surround the Clyde Estuary. My maternal grandfather, John Birch, was a successful artist and he and my grandmother joined us on the trip. The lack of accommodation aboard was partly alleviated by my father sleeping ashore in a tent whenever the boat was moored alongside the land. At the end of the season, with the weather deteriorating, it was decided to leave the boat in

Paisley in the care of Chippy who promised to carry out many improvements during the winter months.

My family returned south to Cornwall for the winter. Unfortunately Chippy failed to live by his word and the boat simply spent the winter lying in the mud in the River Cart, neglected and unattended. That seems to have been the end of Chippy and in the spring the work was carried out by my father alone. During that period the boat got its formal name. Until then it had had none but in his book my father described how *Migrant* was chosen and how John Birch had painted a most beautiful name board showing a flight of mallard ducks against a sky that made use of the grain of the wood. That painting, which accompanied my father on all his subsequent trips to sea and my own trips later, still decorates the walls at home.

With improving weather and most of the work completed the family group embarked again. Once more John Birch arrived with his mountain of painting and fishing gear and we set off to visit more of the lochs. Amongst these was Loch Riddon (see figure 2) that is reached through the Kyles of Bute. Later, in a holiday just before the World War, my Mother and I stayed there at a farm and such things as the daily visit of the paddle steamer and the smell of the seaweed along the shore remain lingering memories. Still, much later in the 1990s, when I had a large yacht myself, we visited Loch Riddon, to find the place much unchanged. At one point I was able to sketch from the same spot where my grandfather had painted so many years before. All that was changed was that the gorse had grown taller. In the second year *Migrant* visited some of the more western lochs, including Loch Goil, before in mid June we entered the Crinan Canal. This picturesque canal cuts off the long finger of the Mull of Kintyre and from the relative shelter of the Clyde Estuary one enters the more turbulent waters of the West coast. From Crinan at the canal's western end, *Migrant* moved up the coast towards Oban. The tidal currents run very fiercely and navigation becomes more demanding. The boat passed through a narrow channel that separates the Isle of Seil and the Scottish mainland. This was an area I was to visit several times in later years as we had close friends living on the island. You can only go through this channel with a boat the size of *Migrant* at the top of the tide. As you look into the clear water beneath the boat you can see the long fronds of kelp waving in the current. There must be something fascinating in this because when I was growing up in boats in Cornwall the sight of kelp under the water always sent a shiver down my spine. At one point on this narrow channel it is crossed by a high arched bridge, called the Clachan Seil, stated to be the only bridge across the Atlantic. A few years ago we bought a little painting of this bridge by Neil Pinket, who though a Cornish based artist, has spent much time painting in that part of the World. On the island side of this bridge is a pub called the Tigh and Truish where the Highlanders are reputed to have changed from kilts to trousers as they were not permitted to wear kilts on the mainland of Scotland during the period of the Jacobite rebellions of 1688-1746. On the western side of the Isle of Seil and a short fifteen minute walk from the pub is a well known yachting anchorage, called the Pulodobrain (pool of the otters). Most of the time it is quiet and idyllic but in strong westerly winds it can become a maelstrom with yachts dragging their anchors, as I discovered later for myself. Further north is Oban, an important hub on that part of the coast with the well known MacBrains steamers sailing from there to all parts of the Western Isles. It is also a magnet for tourists and my father writes rather disparagingly, that even the sausages are dressed in tartan! My grandparents, who had braved the discomforts of living on a small boat, left us at Oban. During their two seasons aboard the *Migrant my* grandfather had painted many pictures and illustrations for my father's book. He had also fished for trout in the various lochs and rivers along the way as he was an avid fisherman, a pursuit that he was to pass to me in the years ahead. Looking back I wonder how my grandparents had stood up to the rather cramped conditions aboard. They were used to the comforts of their house in Cornwall and normally travelled in style. Their departure did at least give some room to house the young nanny. From Oban we headed up the Sound of Mull to Tobermory. From Tobermory we went across the Sound to Loch Sunnart, where bad weather and the declining health of my mother was to bring a final curtain to our voyaging and my own first seagoing experience. On return to Tobermory she consulted a doctor to be told she had tuberculosis. This was a terrifying disease at that time and made a major change to the family's circumstances, although my mother did in fact live to the good age of 85.

School Years

My mother moved to a sanatorium at Midhurst in Sussex and would remain there for the best part of a year. During that time one of her lungs was collapsed but she survived to return to live in Cornwall. However it presented some difficult problems for my father. He had to look after his four year old son and still make a living by writing books. My mother's health must have been a huge worry as the treatment of tuberculosis can be looked at much more positively today than it was then. Fortunately, a great-aunt of mine, Anne Vivian, came to the rescue and very kindly agreed to look after me at St Petroc's Preparatory School that she half owned in Bude, Cornwall. Aunt Anne was one of the Vivian family from which my grandmother Houghton also came. The Vivians are scattered throughout West Cornwall and had much to do with the development of mining machinery for the extraction of tin during the nineteenth century. This was my Cornish connection of which I became justly proud. So it was that my schooling started and days of living away from home and my parents began when I was only four years old! St Petroc's School had about sixty boarders and a lesser number of day boys. My aunt was really the administrator and her partner, a Miss Cherrill, was responsible for the academic side, which included a strong emphasis on religion based on the Church of England faith. Looking back on those years at St Petroc's I realise what a good school it must have been . The Headmaster was Julius Zambra, who directed both the academic and sporting activities of the students. He was an athletic man and was tough with the students. In those days the cane across the backside was permitted and quite regularly used. A summons to the Headmaster's office could be followed by a good six of the best and I and most of the students suffered from this punishment at times. The academic programme was classical with all the traditional subjects of reading, writing and arithmetic. Latin was taught along with French and a limited amount of Greek. English literature and grammar were well covered. This included a strong portion of poetry and many of these poems have kept with me to this day. These included such romantic poems as The *Highwayman* (Alfred Noyes) and *Young Lochinvar rode out of the West* (Sir Walter Scott). It seems likely that the teaching of mathematics did not go into the depth it might have done and I have no recollection of being taught either chemistry or physics. Considering that after leaving this preparatory school I went on to a training ship for the Merchant Navy on which I was interested in very little else other than nautical subjects I am exceedingly grateful for how much of the St Petroc's teaching prepared me with a wider spread of academic knowledge in later years.

Driven by the Headmaster, the school had a strong sports programme. Football, that is soccer, and cricket had a strong emphasis and although I felt that I was not particularly good at either I ended up playing for the first eleven teams in both games and even for a while was captain of the football team. During the war years, several good schools had been evacuated to the vicinity of Bude and so there were some good teams with which to compete. Some fine playing fields were owned by the school and summer evenings could be spent in the cricket nets or practicing catching. Bude, being on the coast, offered opportunities for swimming and there were two salt water pools within easy walking distance of the school. There was also the sea itself but there are strong rip currents at places along the Bude beaches and care had to be taken when swimming in the sea. Surfing in those days was done on plywood boards, although I do not remember being particularly enthusiastic about it. Our range of interests, apart from the formal school sports and academic activities was wide. The Second World War was in full swing and interest from the war, such as making model aircraft, was keen. We were also interested in more peaceful activities and were encouraged to participate in various nature studies, some of which might be frowned upon today. The students collected butterflies and moths and pinned them up for display. They also collected caterpillars and would get greatly excited when they found hawk moth caterpillars of various varieties, particularly when they saw them through to chrysalis and moths. Many of the students became interested in ornithology and I and others with any drawing ability would capture the birds in our sketch books.

In Bude we saw little of the war except for the massing of American troops as they prepared themselves for the invasion of Europe. They introduced us to baseball and some of their American life style. On one occasion a cargo ship carrying supplies for American PX stores collided with an oil tanker off the coast off Bude and much of the cargo was washed ashore. The American troops waded out into the oil covered surf to recover the PX items and give them to the locals, including the students, although the UK Customs considered this as smuggling and did its best to prevent it. Occasionally the sirens would sound and at the school the boys would all be mustered in one of the school corridors until the all clear sounded. Few bombs were actually dropped in the area of Bude, although some of the students had parents living in London and other urban centres that were suffering the severe blitz. Furthermore a number of the children had parents actually involved in the war, including my own father, who was in the navy. Later in the war, when my mother had returned from the sanatorium I would go home for the holidays. In those days petrol was severely rationed and few people had cars so the journey was made by train. This was a great adventure because to go from Bude to Penzance took the best part of a day and required several changes of train. On the route through Okehampton and Plymouth the boys could see all the devastation of Plymouth caused by the bombing. On one occasion HMS *Exeter,* HMS *Ajax* and HMS *Achilles,* which had won great recognition at the Battle of the Plate, were pointed out to us. This caused great excitement! On another occasion we counted the number of churches that had been destroyed through the bombing and counted seventy seven. The almost mandatory requirement today to go home at half terms was not open to the students and so we spent long periods without seeing our parents.

With a strong religious background the students had

regular morning and evening prayers at the school. On Sundays we would walk the mile or so to St Michael's Church, which was across the canal on the other side of the town. It practiced a high Anglican Church form of services and St Petroc's provided the choir. For a period I was the head choir boy at the church. This was the start of a life time interest in singing. Incense was used profusely and for a time I was a boat boy and had to carry the reserve supply of incense in a small silver bowl. During my preparation for confirmation I began to exhibit my first questioning of religion by beginning to query the various beliefs of the Christian faith. My parents' own division of beliefs may have been responsible for my own ambivalent views. My mother was a catholic, although in those days not a particularly strong one and my father was an agnostic, although to his credit he was more Christian in his behaviour than the average person. The weekly walks across the town provided an opportunity to cross the Bude canal, which was always a source of interest. Occasionally, a lovely old Bristol Channel ketch called the *Tralee* would mount the big locks bringing coal from South Wales. On my birthday in May my Aunt Vivian would treat me by inviting another boy and going for a row in the traditional rowing boats that were then available for hire on the canal.

Lamorna

My original home was in West Cornwall. My birth certificate states that I was born in London in Chelsea in 1933, but I like to think that I was conceived in Cornwall, in Nantewas in

Lamorna, a small village near the Land's End where my parents lived before the adventure of sailing in Scotland. The family also lived in the village of Paul. On my mother's discharge from the sanatorium we returned to live again in that part of the country, where my father followed his career as a writer and my mother as a painter. In 1938 the family moved into a house above Mousehole. The village was at that time an active fishing harbour and my father would go down to the quayside each day to yarn with the fishermen and speculate on if and when a conflict was coming. Before it actually started in September 1939 my father decided to join the Merchant Navy and went off on a ship bound for Australia. Mousehole, as well as Lamorna, had active artists' colonies which appealed to my mother's interests. With the actual declaration of war the family was obliged to move out of Mousehole. This was probably because the house was rented from a farmer and under the wartime rules farmers could evict tenants from agricultural land. As it was the family moved into a bungalow with a fine view of Newlyn harbour. Looking down on the port we would often see French and Belgian fishing boats arriving that had escaped from Nazi occupied Europe. On arrival the boats would be boarded by navy personnel to check the credentials of the crews and see that they were not illegally infiltrating into the country. During those years in Mousehole and later in Newlyn I was away during the term times at St Petroc's School in Bude. My father had joined the Merchant Navy but was later to transfer to the Royal Navy Volunteer Reserve (RNVR).

Lamorna's rich industrial and artistic heritage helped to shape my earlier years. Towards the end of the war in 1944 my maternal grandmother Houghton or Mouse as she was nick named, died of cancer and my mother and I moved to Lamorna to provide support for my grandfather, the successful artist Samuel John Lamorna Birch, who by that time was a Royal Academician. Prior to that we had regularly travelled to Lamorna and had spent weekends with my maternal grandparents at Flagstaff Cottage. Lamorna was, and remains a magical place. In a steep valley facing south it is well sheltered from the prevailing westerly winds and has an almost sub-tropical climate. A small trout stream runs through it and at its seaward end there is a small cove with a granite quay that had been originally built for the purpose of shipping out the granite that was quarried in the valley. In spite of its beauty, Lamorna has been subjected over the years to various types of commercial activity. There has always been a mixture of dairy and arable farming in the open fields above the valley. Until recently a small amount of inshore commercial fishing has been based in the sheltered cove.

The first major industrial activity was the tin streaming that had started in the thirteenth century. The main tin lode in this part of Cornwall is on the northern coast, from St Just to Pendeen. Long before deep shaft mining had been started in that area, the erosion of this tin carried it southwards to valleys such as Lamorna as sediments in the rivers and streams. The process of extracting the placer tin was to continually divert the stream and its tributaries, panning through the sediments of each new passage of the water. The heritage of this industry can be seen today in the woods bordering the stream and along the narrow flood plain, as mounds of boulders, now covered with vegetation. Between these mounds there are dry water courses and stagnant ponds. A few remnants of small granite buildings are all that remains to directly show man's activities. Tin streaming did not always fit in well with the adjacent farming activities as there was competition for the use of the land and the water that ran through it. A case of this conflict has been described by a local author Jim Hosking[1] where a sixteen year law suit followed the death of a tinner during a dispute in 1387.

The second industrial activity to take place on the east side of the valley was quarrying for granite beginning about 1800. The large tips of the rejected granite chippings are still clearly visible today. Lamorna for a time produced some very fine stone that was quarried and shipped to places such as the Thames where the granite was used to build the Embankment. It was also used to build breakwaters in Alderney and Portland. In 1851 an obelisk that was 22 feet in height and weighed 21 tons was sent to the Great Exhibition but whether it still exists today is not known. Although the big quarry immediately above the Cove is today the most distinctive there were in fact several quarries along the length of the valley. A problem was to move the hewn granite to market and in the earlier years it was taken on large wagons towed by teams of horses over the hill to

[1] Jim Hosking, *People and Places in Paul Parish*, 2005.

load on ships in the port of Newlyn. This is well recorded in a fine painting *The Quarry Team*, 1894 by Stanhope Forbes RA. Some attempts were made to load the granite directly on to ships from portable structures on the east side of the stream but this must have been difficult and precarious. A rival company decided to quarry on the west side of the Cove but having built a magnificent infrastructure in 1854, comprising the granite quay, the hotel and harbour master's cottage, it was found that the granite was flawed due to the occurrence of quartz veins and that quarry was abandoned.

The third activity was the arrival of the artists. This took place in about 1900, just as the quarries were closing. Led by my grandfather, who came to Cornwall from Lancaster in northern England in 1892, a thriving art colony was established. The Newlyn School of Art had been formed some twenty years earlier but Lamorna provided an offshoot for those artists who were more interested in landscape painting than the carefully posed models in a fishing village background that were the prime subject of the Newlyn School. The Lamorna School attracted a group of artists in the period between 1902 and 1914 that was to include several successful painters that in addition to my Grandfather included Sir Alfred Munnings, who later became the President of the Royal Academy and Laura and Harold Knight, both of whom were to become well known Academicians. Although less in number than the painters there have also been a number of writers who have lived in the village over the years. These include Crosbie Garstin, who wrote a trilogy of books about the fictitious life of the

Penhale family that lived in Lamorna in the eighteenth century and Derek Tangye, who lived on the coast and sought a simple life growing daffodils and writing stories about animals and birds. A resident in more recent times has been the writer John LeCarre, (David Cornwell) who I occasionally meet today walking the coastal path and who owns a house on the cliffs at nearby Tregiffian. My own father added to the number of writers when he returned from the War. This active centre of creative art during the early years of the twentieth century led to the construction, by the wealthier artists, of several of the fine granite houses that can be seen today hidden amongst the trees. Finally as the artists became less active, tourism began to take over and continues to this day. This description of Lamorna's industrial and artistic past may seem unnecessary but it provides the background into which I moved and was to pass my formative years.

The social structure of the village has greatly changed. When I grew up in Lamorna the class structure was clearly apparent. There were the working class labourers who worked on the nearby farms or farmed their own cliff top fields growing early potatoes and flowers. This latter activity was extremely hard work as the fields were small enclosures, usually on sloping ground, facing the sea. All the produce had to be hand carried up the hills to a point where a wagon could reach them. In the lower valley, closer to the stream, the fields were owned by farmers that could afford to hire labourers themselves. There was a limited amount of fishing in small boats from the Cove. The amount of fishing activity rose and fell with the stocks available and the market prices. Most of the fishermen worked as farm labourers during the day and as fishermen in the early mornings and evenings. At the end of the war there were several professional families, some shopkeepers, who commuted from Penzance and retired people. All of these formed a middle class. Artists could not be classified and seemed to move easily within whatever structure existed. Today the social structure is much changed with the community mainly comprised of retired people, or professional people who commute into Penzance or Truro or work at home with the Internet. A limited number of professional artists exist today by having some other occupation, such as teaching to sustain them financially. The social structure must have been of interest to my father, who had moved to Cornwall from the Scottish Clyde with strong working class socialistic views. My grandfather on the other hand had also moved from a working class background in Lancashire but seems to have quickly taken on the conservative views of the countryman. I remember that at elections my family was evenly split between my mother favouring my father's socialist views and supporting the Labour party and my grandfather and our Cornish housekeeper supporting the Conservatives or perhaps the Liberals.

On being demobbed after the war my father (1899-1963)[2] returned to live with his family in Lamorna. His first task

---

[2] Stephen Bigger, University of Worcester 2007

was to rebuild a hut that my grandfather had provided for a fisherman, old John Jefferies. Once the hut was completed my father set out to re-establish himself as an author, primarily of sea stories. He said that those authors who had not gone to war were able to maintain their contacts and readership but he must have gathered much experience from his war experiences. He wrote under two pen names and his own James Lennox Kerr. For serious historical books and novels he used his own name, books written for boys were written under Peter Dawlish and thrillers under Gavin Douglas.

Before the War my father had written several serious novels based on working class Scotland[3] and on his experiences in Australia and North America.[4] He had written a series of books, intended for a young audience, about a fictitious Captain Samson and another series about Captain Peg-Leg.[5] He was much impressed by Arthur Ransome and developed a line of boys' books around the activities of a group of young boys and a Breton fishing vessel that they had found abandoned on a Cornish beach and had re-built. I probably provided a model for him because at that time I was about 12, the age of the boys in his books. During his career as a writer he had over fifty books published.

His boys' books, particularly *the Dauntless Series* written under Peter Dawlish, were steady but modest sellers. He wrote several books that were of an autobiographical

---

[3] For example, Lennox Kerr, *Glenshiels*, The Bodley Head Ltd, 1933

[4] Lennox Kerr, *Back Door Guest,* Constable and Co Ltd, 1930

[5] Peter Dawlish, *Captain Peg-Legs War*, Oxford University Press, 1939

nature, particularly *Eager Years*, which described his life up to the age of thirty. Starting from very modest beginnings in Scotland he had had an exciting and varied life that was mainly associated with the sea. He had spent periods in both Australia and the USA, after having 'jumped his ship'. During these times ashore he had been involved in everything from being a hobo in America to teaching ballroom dancing to a boxer in Australia. He had spent time on a Hudson Bay ship in the Arctic and used this experience to write *Ice*[6]. He eventually came ashore to live in London in 1930 determined to become a writer. It was then that he met my mother and this led to their marriage in 1932 in St Ives, Cornwall.

My father spent most of the war in command of minesweepers but during the invasion of Europe he was appointed to command a landing craft tank (LCT) During the invasion he was employed in landing American troops and their tanks on Omaha Beach. Although not promoted beyond a lieutenant in the RNVR, throughout the war he was mentioned in dispatches. At the end of the war he returned to the minesweeper and mine-laying and on being demobbed he returned to his life as a writer, living with his family at Lamorna.

During the war years I had not spent much time with my father and most of my parenting fell on the shoulders of my mother. My grandfather filled the void as a male role model by encouraging my interest in trout fishing, a general love of

---

[6] Lennox Kerr, *Ice*, The Bodley Head Ltd, 1933.

nature, drawing and sketching. Sadly, although he did show me some of the basic skills of the water colourist, such as the use of cobalt washes to show distance and the general importance of tonal differences, I should have spent more time gaining this important knowledge.

When my father returned after the war he quickly set about giving his own spin to my development and association with the sea. Although he must have been very busy re-establishing his own career he spent much time teaching me the everyday skills of the sailor, such as tying bends and hitches and he also built my first boat. This was a very strong flat bottomed punt, ten feet in length that we could launch in the harbour at Lamorna. In this I learnt the basic skills of rowing, sculling and manoeuvring the boat.

Figure 3 My little *Fulmar.*

A year later he introduced me to sailing after converting a 12 foot boat with a lug sail and a centre board called the *Fulmar.* This was the start of my life long interest in both recreational and professional sailing. The die had been cast and I was set to be a sailor rather than an artist, although an interest in art has remained throughout my life and sea going career.

HMS *Conway*

When I was twelve my father wrote to me proposing that after leaving St Petroc's I could either apply to join HMS *Conway*, a training ship for officers in the Merchant Navy or go to a Technical High School in Ayrshire in Scotland. He held strong views as a socialist and although he was happy for me to attend my great aunt's preparatory school he did not want me to go on to a public school. My grandfather had kindly agreed to pay for the secondary education of all his grand children so money was not the issue but my father did not want me to follow the pattern of going on to a public school, which in his opinion, produced arrogant snobs. In the case of St Petroc's most of the boys went on to West Country public schools, such as Blundells or Kelly College. The

Figure 4 HM School ship *Conway*.

Ayrshire option reflected his admiration for the Scottish education system but if you ask a twelve year boy if he would like to go to sea or to a technical institution he will most probably choose the former. That was the choice I made, a decision that was to have a major impact on my future life.

Figure 5 Adam Kerr dressed and ready to join the *Conway*, aged thirteen.

HMS *Conway* was a floating school that had originally been HMS *Nile*, a two deck 92-gun second-rate that had been renamed in 1872. Previously it had been anchored at Rock Ferry, off Liverpool, but during the war it had been moved to the greater safety of North Wales and was on a permanent mooring off Bangor. It was rigged as a three masted ship but this was much reduced and carried no sail, or did the ship move off its mooring. With Britain's merchant fleet at its peak there was a need to produce well educated young officers and there were at that time three similar institutions, the *Conway,* the *Worcester* and *Pangbourne.* Students between the ages of 13½ and 16½ joined these schools for two years as cadets. At the end of that period they would join a shipping company and go to sea as an apprentice or midshipman as they were called in the smarter companies, for a further three years.

Young men going to sea without attending these institutions would serve four years as an apprentice. At the end of that time they could study for and write exams for second mate and they were then qualified as junior officers.

Having made the decision in my last year at St Petroc's to go to the *Conway,* my school curriculum had to be quickly changed. I could give up the much hated Latin classes and concentrate on a higher level of mathematics. I would be thirteen when I left St Petroc's and had yet to study calculus. The days moved quickly and early in 1947 I was ready to join my training ship. Uniforms had to be ordered and worn at all times. I can vividly remember the struggles to get on the shirt and separate collar attached by studs, a battle that later became routine. My parents drove me up to North Wales and took me aboard the ship on one of its launches but were quickly encouraged to leave. There I was, aged 13, rather short for my age and struggling to adapt to this completely foreign environment where many of the cadets spoke with strong north-country dialects!

The ship was to be my home and school room for the next two years. We slept in hammocks at night and during the day partitions were lowered to convert the decks into mess rooms and class rooms. Everything moved to the call of a bugle, whether it was reveille, slack party (a punishment group) or the last post. All one's belongings had to be kept in a wooden sea chest and the cadets were responsible for ensuring that their uniforms were always well kept and the holes in their socks were darned. Discipline was maintained by the uniformed officers but most of the school subjects were taught by civilians, brought out by boat each day from the shore. We had great respect for the officers but little respect for the civilian teachers and nothing pleased us more than to see the teachers getting soaked with sea water on rough days as they arrived in the launches.

The school work was a mixture of normal school subjects, such as mathematics, English and a foreign language – Spanish and various nautical subjects, such as navigation, seamanship and engineering. As the interest was in becoming sailors the nautical subjects drew the greatest attention from the students. There were two hundred cadets living aboard and they were divided into *tops*. This was similar to school houses but they were named for parts of a warship's rigging, such as mizzen top, main top and foretop. Each top was led and disciplined by a senior and a junior cadet captain. Discipline was reinforced by the use of 'teasers'. These were a short length of thin rope with a loop at one end and a back splice at the other which could be swung across the backside of the cadets for any infraction. A particular reason for punishment was the unsatisfactory lashing of your hammock when they were stowed in racks during the day. Bullying of the first year students known as 'new chums' was a major occupation of the senior students.

John Masefield, who became the Poet Laureate, had been a *Conway* boy but had not gone to sea. He had written a book in 1945 *New Chum*, which described the hazing aboard and when my mother read it soon after I had joined the ship she was quite terrified. However, in spite of all I survived, to become a senior cadet captain during my last year on the ship, wielding a teaser myself to enforce discipline.

Sporting activities were carried out ashore and included rugby, cricket and athletics. Rowing and sailing were also actively pursued. The Menai Straits, where the ship was moored, is a rough body of water, with strong tidal currents. Rowing was undertaken in heavy naval whalers or cutters. At just under five feet high I was too small to make a good oarsman but ended up as coxswain of the Captain's gig, a finely white painted and varnished rowing boat used for the ceremonial deployment of the Captain. The main competitor in both rugby and rowing was *HMS Worcester*, which was located at Greenhithe on the Thames.

As all transportation to the shore was by boat there were a number of motor and rowing boats. It was a great privilege to be a member of the heavy weather rowing cutter. Appointments as the coxswain or engineer of the motor boats were also much sought after jobs. Each night the boats were either hoisted on the davits by a team of cadets or put out on booms on each side of the ship. It was often rough and I can well remember the launches plunging through the heavy chop that occurred when there were strong winds and strong tides. In the term before I left plans had been made to move the ship and the institution at large through the Menai

Straits and to moor the ship off the Marquis of Anglesey's estate at Plas Newydd. A task in which I participated was moving the very heavy anchors and chains from Bangor to the new site. This involved slinging the heavy gear under the boats and towing the boats through the turbulent Swillies – a constricted part of the Straits, where the currents were particularly strong. After I had left, the ship was towed through the Swillies and moored off Plas Newydd. Sadly a few years later it was decided to take the ship to Liverpool for docking and while under tow by tugs it ran aground under the Menai Bridge and became a total loss.

A particularly good memory of my time on *Conway* was for the boys in their final year to be sent to the Outward Bound Sea School at Aberdovey in West Wales. The boys attending that school ranged from Public School boys to Borstal boys and to many of them the time at Aberdovey was a considerable hardship. However for the *Conway* boys it was a huge release from the confines and tight discipline of our ship. The Outward Bound School had an active programme of physical education in the form of many sporting activities and strong competition. There was also a fleet of small boats and a busy sailing programme. A specific part of that was to spend a week on a ketch called the *Garibaldi*. For most of us sea sickness was an associated part of that experience. I can also remember being told by the Welsh mate to 'stop that bloody whistling, you will bring a gale of wind!' On weekends the boys would go on long treks through the beautiful mountainous country of West Wales. A final epic hike was over 40 miles. A treat for the boys who had been living on the bland food aboard *Conway* was to walk several miles inland to Blwch farm to enjoy heaped plates of bacon and eggs.

Back on the *Conway* some of the brighter parts of life can be recalled. Once a year there was a ball on board to which the ladies of Bangor University were invited. As the age of *Conway* cadets ranged from 13½ to 18½ the Bangor students were rather older than most of the cadets, certainly as one of the younger cadets and my short stature I might not have been as impressive to the girls as I might have wished. However, it must have been a glamorous occasion for the Bangor University students to come aboard and enjoy the maritime flavour. The decks of the ship would be all dressed up with flags and the brass would be well polished. All our guests had to be ferried aboard in the launches and that was probably in itself a thrill for them. Another memory was the communal singing when the entire ship's company would gather around the large hatchway in the middle of the ship to sing romantic old songs, such as 'Now is the Hour.' To participate in the singing and being part of the large throng of cadets was an emotional and moving experience.

After spending two years aboard it was time to say good-bye. Most of the cadets signed on to go to sea with some of the better shipping companies. Although the programme was mainly directed at providing Merchant Navy officers, there was a small group that were directed towards a late entry into the Royal Navy. Cadets in the navy programme were required to have a good academic record. I discussed the possibility of joining the navy programme with my father but he had said 'You don't want to join the navy as it is a boring occupation in peace time!' As much later in life I brushed shoulders continually with hydrographic surveyors, who were senior naval officers and some of them even admirals, one wonders where I would have ended up if I had followed that course. As far as the Merchant Navy cadets were concerned, those with better marks usually went to the smarter shipping companies, such as P & O or the Royal Mail Line, while the ones with lower marks ended up in tanker companies. Things have changed and no doubt today the Master of a Super tanker is a desirable occupation. The Blue Funnel Line or Alfred Holt & Co, as it was properly called, a large Liverpool based company, did much financially to support the *Conway,* and employed a large share of the graduating cadets. This ended up as my choice, probably because my socialist father encouraged me not to join a posh liner company but a company with hard working cargo liners.

A Gap Year

I joined *Conway* at the earliest possible age of 13½ and spent two years aboard as a cadet making me 15½ when I left in 1949. Normally I would then spend 3 years as an apprentice. The second mate's ticket could not be taken until you were 20 so I had time in hand and it was decided by my father that I should spend the year gaining some different experience. Today we would call this a gap year. My father tried to get me a place on the four-masted barque, *Pamir,* which was one of the famous P line square riggers that were then under the German flag. This did not prove possible and in fact only a few years later the ship was lost in a hurricane with all hands. As an alternative he worked out a programme for me to spend time on variety of smaller ships.

Before embarking on that programme I accompanied my parents on a trip on the Dutch canals – my first foreign experience. During the war my father had met a man who said that if he wanted a job after the war he should make contact with him. Instead the man took the initiative and offered my father a job as the Staff Captain on a small cruise ship in a company called Yacht Holidays. This was really the start of an industry that has today become huge. The vessels were mainly retired naval MLs (Motor Launches) that had been cleverly converted to small passenger carrying vessels with space aboard for about 20 passengers. My family was offered a test cruise. We were met at Liverpool Station in London by a courier and then travelled first class to Harwich where we joined the ferry that sailed to the Hook of Holland. At the terminal we were met by limousines that took us to join the little ship at Maasluis. We then spent a week cruising the canals in the northern part of Holland, visiting cities such as Dortrecht, Amsterdam, Haarlem and The Hague. The passengers would cruise the canals looking out from a lounge at the passing Dutch scenery and there were various side trips to see local scenery and sites. My own trip was made brighter by having as fellow passengers two beautiful girls from what was then Southern Rhodesia. As we made up the youngest passengers on board we had some good times together and I have wondered what happened to them and if they returned to what is now Zimbabwe. At the end of the pleasant and very impressionable week, we returned to England by the same route. As there was the potential for friction between the experienced Dutch skipper, who navigated the little ship and my father as the Staff Captain, my father decided to decline the job offer.

Next, it was arranged that I should spend some time on a trawler in the North Sea. During the war my father had got to know a fellow skipper of minesweepers who was a trawler skipper in peace time. I travelled to Grimsby to join the boat which was fishing on the Dogger Bank. The skipper looked after me as well as he could but for half of the nine days at sea I was badly sea sick. Every few hours the trawl would be hauled in and on the release of the cod end, the re-enforced net at the end of the net, a cascade of fish emptied on the deck, much of the fish being prime fish such as turbot, sole and cod. The crew then had to sort and gut the fish, all very hard, wet and smelly work. After the War the North Sea was teeming with fish and the catches were large. I remember that the crew themselves would choose gurnards to eat, presumably as the prime fish such as soles and turbot had a good market value but gurnard although good to eat had a low market value. After the net rose up through the water many small fish and debris floated clear and large tuna could be seen dashing through the nearby water and hoovering them up. I once asked the engineer to make me a big hook and attached this to a heavy line with a mackerel for bait but it was no sooner in the water than it was snapped up and the line broken by a passing tuna.

My next trip was as a cabin boy on a small coaster from Falmouth to Spain. The first adventure was to tow a broken down motor torpedo boat that was being illegally delivered to Israel, into Vigo on the northwest Spanish coast. In that port I met a group of boys about my own age and was taken by them to see my first bull fight. I was also taken to a brothel by some of the crew, an experience to remember, although I do not recall participating in its delights! We went down the coast of Portugal and entered a river that was the southern boundary between Portugal and Spain. Our purpose of going there was to load iron ore in a small town on the Guadiana River. The crew amused themselves by acquiring numerous tortoises, which were abundant in that area. So that they did not lose them as they wandered about the deck they painted them white. Whether they eventually got their freedom in some pleasant English field or ended up having to swim for their lives I do not know

On return from the Spanish trip I was given a place on the Trinity House lighthouse service vessel *Satellite* that was based in Penzance. The ship carried supplies to the lighthouses and serviced the buoys around the Cornish coast. We visited several of the major lighthouses and enjoyed the exciting business of being swung up to the platform on a rope skipping across the waves. During my time aboard I was able to watch how the lighthouse keepers fished with a kite off the Eddystone lighthouse so as to carry the baited line into the deeper water and clear of the lighthouse structure. The *Satellite* supplied the main lighthouses around the Scilly Isles, including Round Island, the isolated Wolf Rock and Bishop Rock Lighthouses. Later in my career I became a Younger Brother of Trinity House and visited many of these navigational beacons in another capacity.

The mate on the *Satellite* was an interesting man called Kendall-Carpenter. Although he dearly loved the sea he never succeeded in getting the necessary qualification and never became a Captain, which must have been a great disappointment to him. He was a great supporter of Trinity House and after his retirement took part in all its ceremonial events. In the years since my time on that ship the organisation has greatly streamlined its fleet and now has only two ships that are so large they are unable to enter Penzance and the smaller ports. Today all the lighthouses are unmanned and much of the servicing is done by helicopters.

My final trip of that eventful summer was to spend some time on one of the last working Thames Sailing barges, based at Greenhithe in the Thames. This large sailing vessel did not have an engine and I was able to see the two man crew manoeuvre this large vessel. The crew was made up of a thirty year old skipper and his sixteen year old brother – my own age at the time. Most of the barge was used for the cargo and there was a small cabin at the after end where there were two bunks that could be closed off with doors. The barge moved up and down the Thames by the wind when it was available and took advantage of the tidal currents which are strong in parts of the river. To control the direction of the boat as it was carried up and down the river by the tidal currents a technique called kedging was sometimes employed, in which the anchor is lowered so that it is just touching the bottom and allows the helmsman to steer the barge back and forth across the channel. 1949 was a warm summer and the Thames River was extremely polluted. The kedging process stirred up the smelly bottom sediments. In fact the pollution had the effect of changing the white painted parts of the woodwork blue! During the few weeks spent on this boat we travelled up to the Royal Docks with bags of fertiliser to be loaded on board ships and sailed down to the Isle of Sheppey with smelly hides for a tannery. The boy and I were together aboard most of the time with the skipper going home at night from wherever the boat ended up at the end of the day. The boy and I were not the greatest of friends, coming from greatly different backgrounds and values but he provided me with some very different insights of life. The boy had learnt his skilled trade by serving his apprenticeship on this last of the working sailing vessel on the Thames while I had spent my time on a large training ship destined to give me the knowledge to start on my own apprenticeship as a foreign going sailor. There can be no doubt that at that time he was the master and I was the student. In recent years I have found myself in

Faversham in Kent and met some of the crews of the old sailing barges that still exist and admired their sailing skills. I wonder if my old companion is amongst them and still carrying out his trade on the river, although it will be paying passengers and not cargoes that are carried. Sadly I have been unable to discover the name of the sailing barge on which I spent some interesting weeks.

The final part of my gap year was ashore as a student at the Penzance Arts' School. My programme was arranged by its principal, an etcher called Bouverie Hoyton. I was taught design by a well known designer and surrealist painter called John Tunnard . I tried my hand at throwing and decorating pots, although I was always frustrated by the process of centring a lump of clay on the spinning wheel. Perhaps to keep me amused, Bouverie had me make a large model of a sailing ship like the *Conway*. As I was only sixteen, I was not permitted to participate in the nude life classes but spent time drawing clothed models. The art school experience gave me the opportunity for a final few months at home before my seagoing career. It also wetted my appetite for art and I have remained a keen amateur water colourist throughout my life but was never brave enough to 'swallow the anchor' and make my living as an artist instead of a sailor. Nevertheless my sketchbook has accompanied me through all my travels and these include drawings done from the Antarctic to the Arctic, in fine weather and bad. Mostly these have been landscapes or seascapes as the drawing of figures has never been a strong point. I have stuck mainly to watercolours on account of their portability but have tried most of the common media of oil, acrylics and etching. From time to time I have sold my work but the main reason for the occupation is that it simply takes you away from everything else as you become absorbed in observing the world in front of you and trying to convert the scene to an image on paper or board.

EARLY DAYS AS A DEEP WATER SAILOR

Blue Funnel Line Years

The date on which I signed my indentures as an apprentice with the Blue Funnel Line on 6 January, 1950 remains etched in my mind. This contract, entrenched in history, stated that the apprentice was not to enter taverns, ale houses or places of ill repute! For this I was to receive the princely sum of £6.50 a month. The offices of the Blue Funnel Line or Alfred Holt & Co were in the Liver Buildings, besides the Mersey River. When asked on my first interview what was my ambition the correct answer was to say that it was to be the Master of a Blue Funnel liner. That eventuality was many years in the future because at that time, although you may have become qualified as a foreign-going master mariner around your mid twenties it was likely that you would only become a Master when you were around forty. Alfred Holt & Co included two shipping companies, the Blue Funnel line and the Glen line. The ships of the two companies were almost identical in appearance except that the funnels of Glen Line ships were painted red with a black top and those of the Blue Funnel Line ships were painted blue with a black top. Glen Line ships also tended to sail out of London rather than Liverpool. Ship's officers could find themselves on either of the company's ships and the apprentices were called midshipmen. During time in Liverpool waiting for our ships the midshipmen would usually be quartered in a house ashore, colloquially called the 'Holt's Baby Farm', joining their ships just before sailing time. Blue Funnel ships berthed in either the Gladstone docks on the Liverpool side or in Birkenhead. I always remember sailing in and out of Liverpool with its rather gloomy weather. The ship would be locked out of the harbour confines and then down river and out to sea across the Bar. A pilot would take the ship as far as Holyhead. The ships were mainly assigned on lines to the Far East, with a few going to Australia and one or two going to ports in the USA.

Figure 6 SS *Machaon*, Adam's first Ship.

The route to the Far East was well trodden. The courses took the ship through the Straits of Gibraltar and then through the Suez Canal. Passing through the canal the ships were mustered in groups and at points the south bound convoy had to tie up to the bank to allow the north bound convoy to pass. This involved the crew standing by the mooring lines and at night I was very surprised to find how cold the desert became compared with the heat of the midday sun. The route was then down the Red Sea, with sometimes a stop at Aden to pick up fuel. On my first trip to sea on a coal burning ship called *Machaon,* the coaling took place in Aden. It was brought to the ship in barges and was then carried in baskets by gangs of men who had to walk up a narrow plank. An Arab overseer in a white robe cracked a long stock whip to urge the stevedores to move faster on their task. It was then across the Indian Ocean to Penang, where the smell of the tropical vegetation as we approached the low coastline of Malaya remains a distinctive memory. After Penang we called at Port Swettenham (now Klang) and on to Singapore. At Penang a crowd of many coloured stevedores come aboard to work the ship. Black tamils, brown Malays who seemed to work on the less physical jobs, such as tally clerks, and wizened Chinese, who I was told were mainly heroin drug addicts. From Singapore most of the trips went north to Hong Kong, stopping at the company's big facilities at Kowloon, then onwards to Japan, or to different places in East Asia including Chinese mainland ports, and to the Philippines. During my time with the company the Korean war was in progress and the Chinese Communists were at odds with the Nationalists. As the Blue Funnel ships traded into both mainland China and Taiwan there were incidents with ships being attacked and so many ships had a union jack painted on their hatches to make their nationality quite clear.

Figure 7 Adam Kerr, MV *Phemius*, watercolour.

Although some of the Blue Funnel and Glen line ships were on very precise scheduled voyages, lasting one hundred days to the Far East, some of its fastest and best ships were on the Australian route, making quick voyages of about five months and calling at all the major Australian ports.

Most of the ships carried twelve passengers, the limit before a doctor had to be carried, but the large Australian ships could carry up to forty passengers. The company had an ambivalent policy about the intermingling of the ship's officers and the passengers and it depended very much on the will of the Captain.

I got to know some of the passengers who were mostly tea and rubber planters or civil servants going back and forth on holidays. On some ships there would be a firm white line drawn on the deck that separated passengers and crew, including the officers. On those ships the only intermingling was at the Captain's table with the Captain, Chief Engineer and the Doctor representing the company.

During the period from 1950 to 1955, I spent time on eight of the company's ships and travelled extensively throughout the Far East and Australia. Most voyages were less than five months but one trip, on a ship called the *Dolius*, which started as a five months voyage to Australia and back, ended up lasting fourteen months. This took me to Australia but also included two voyages from Australia to Indonesia and Malaya and eventually back to the United Kingdom. In the early trips to Australia in the 1950s there was considerable labour unrest in that country and the stevedores spent many days on strike. This resulted in the ships spending long periods at anchor off Melbourne and Sydney enabling me to see something of the country and in my case to be able to visit my Aunt and Uncle who had emigrated there in the years after the War. Visiting Australia now over 50 years later, several memories come back to remind me how that large country has changed. On a trip to collect frozen meat from an abattoir near Brisbane we were taken to see the inhumane killing of the animals, something that has been greatly changed. During that time the policy of £10 poms resulted in many British and Europeans travelling out to the country on the large P & O Liners. I remember a poll being taken of the stevedores working on the ship of whether Orientals should be allowed to enter the country. The response was then very negative – a far cry from the situation of today.

A particularly memorable couple of voyages were on the *Calchas* to the Far East. This ship was assigned as the company's training vessel and the normal deck crew was entirely made up of midshipmen. There was an elderly boatswain but the crew were managed by the boatswain's mate, who was a midshipman. He was assisted by the lamp trimmer, a traditional title but at that time the man responsible for mixing all the paint and doing all the splicing, both rope and wire. He also helped the boatswain's mate in his supervisory duties. I was fortunate in being assigned as lamp trimmer on my second voyage and it gave me great opportunities to hone up my sailor's skills, such as splicing wire and heavy rope hawsers. The formal title of the job made me responsible for ensuring that the large copper oil lights were permanently full of oil. Happily a break down of the electric supply never happened during my watch.

The cargoes were very varied. Outward bound there was a lot of steel and heavy machinery and with a healthy British automobile industry many cars were being shipped overseas. This included vast numbers of Land Rovers, Austins, Ford Cortinas and Humbers. Spirits were also one of the main cargoes and preventing pilfering was a major task. In British ports during the loading the stevedores would try to break the wooden cases of spirits and to extract a drink or even whole bottles. In Malaya we sometimes carried ingots of tin and this had to be very carefully guarded due to their great value. On voyages from Australia to Indonesia the crew had considerable trouble in preventing the pilfering of the canned fruit cargoes that we carried. The country was quite lawless having not long before achieved independence from the Netherlands. The ships' own crews were not above illegal activity themselves as they quickly found that smuggling ashore a tin of 50 cigarettes could provide payment for a very good night of drinking and the company of beautiful Indonesian girls. The cargoes back through Malaya and Singapore consisted of large quantities of rubber in bales that stuck together if not kept dry and well covered with French chalk. Starting in Japan and moving through Hong Kong there were many cased goods containing toys and other baubles. A final top up of boxes of tea was often made in Ceylon, now Sri Lanka. This posed a complicated stowage as when arriving at ports in northern Europe and the United Kingdom it was desirable to have easy access to particular boxes of the tea. Stowage of this great variety of cargoes was arranged by the chief officer and was a demanding task. Not only did the weight distribution have to be carefully considered but such matters as the order of unloading and of crushing and tainting of adjacent cargo had to be considered. All this was carefully mapped by the chief officer to be made available for the company and those responsible for unloading the ship. The cargo was unloaded in various European ports such as Genoa and Marseilles in the Mediterranean and Rotterdam, Amsterdam, Bremen, Hamburg and Copenhagen in northern Europe. The ships would then move on to complete the discharge in various British ports which included London, Liverpool, Avonmouth and Glasgow. Today the use of containers has greatly simplified the complex stowage problems of general cargoes and no doubt changed the tasks of the chief officers. It has also considerably lessened the pilferage of the cargo or perhaps consolidated pilferage when it occurred to whole containers.

The carriage of animals was usually rewarding for the midshipmen as they were often assigned to look after them and sometimes received a good tip for their care. The carriage of race horses or even circus animals was particularly rewarding. A memorable cargo of that kind was to carry twelve Australian Queensland Healer cattle dogs from Brisbane to Singapore. These dogs were destined for the British Army in Malaya to help it fight the communist forces that were then operating in that country. The dogs came aboard straight from the farms and were very dirty. We had a Chinese crew that was most unkind to the animals blasting them with the salt water hose when they were washing down the decks each morning. We got the dogs' own revenge by securing them on lines where the Chinese crew had to pass on their way to their accommodation. When we arrived at Singapore the British 'tommies' were all lined up on the dock to take on their charges. The Queensland healer at that time was not tightly defined by breed features and the dogs were of greatly varying size. The soldiers who were aboard first got the pick of the larger dogs but the later ones, to their disgust, ended up with very small dogs on which the large muzzles and leads hardly fitted.

Alfred Holt & Co owned over one hundred ships, typically of 10,000 gross tons. The company believed in building very strong ships and they were self insured which meant that everything possible was done to maintain their excellence and prevent accidents. In their construction the company continued to use riveting while most other companies had moved to welding which was starting to make inroads in ship construction technology, but Alfred Holt's ships continued to be of riveted construction because the strength of welding was not trusted. There was a regular programme of maintenance during the voyages and the ships were totally repainted on the homeward voyage. This started by painting the masts in Japan or some other distant port and then gradually painting the whole ship so that it arrived at its home port in Europe looking very smart. Navigation was carried out under strict rules, so much so that we were laughed at by those on ships owned by less demanding companies. There was a precise order book listing every course the ship should take and maintain. In this book courses were prescribed that took the ship well clear of all potential dangers. For example the ships were ordered to keep twenty miles off the dangerous corner of Ushant in northwest France. There was of course no satellite navigation and out of sight of land positioning was achieved by astronomical means. At dawn and dusk, if the weather permitted the chief and fourth officer observed star sights and at noon the Captain and all the officers observed the sun crossing the meridian to obtain latitude. At the end of each four hour watch the officers were required to mark the ship's position on the chart with each officer using a different coloured pencil. After the voyage the charts were scrutinised at the Head Office to ensure that all the positions plotted on the charts had been correctly made. Every officer was supervised by the next rank above him. Although this method of management must have been thoroughly evaluated by the company, particularly in view of its self insurance policy, its effect on the self confidence of the officers may be questioned. Later when I moved to other ships where the officers were given more freedom it seems that they developed greater confidence in their individual capabilities.

During my years at sea with Alfred Holt and Company my father had had discussions with some friends who were partners in a large London legal firm and he become convinced that if as well as having a master's seagoing qualification I could become a barrister and could go on to handle the cases dealing with maritime law for the company. This was to be my first attempt to get involved in legal matters concerning the sea. I went to the Inns of Court to find out what was involved and looked into such matters as participating in the formal dinners. I discovered that to enter the legal profession at that time it was necessary for me to pass exams in Latin. Therefore I took my books to sea and in my spare time tried to learn Latin. I had studied Latin at St Petroc's and was most unsuccessful and this second attempt while I was at sea proved to be no easier or more palatable. For the time being my legal ambitions were stymied.

During my seven years with Blue Funnel I completed the time as an apprentice and came ashore to study for and to pass my Second Mate's certificate. I did this in London, where I studied at the King Edward VII Navigation School and stayed in a club on the Minories called the Seamark. That part of London and to the east was still a sailors' town. Teams of horses still towed wagons full of beer down cobbled streets. The docks were a sea of cranes. There were excellent pubs and even a few music halls, which the young sailors would visit on a good night out to hire a box and heckle the actors. One of the key elements of seagoing qualifications was to know the rules of the road in word perfect manner. When I visit that part of London by the Tower Bridge today I can remember the hours spent on a bench overlooking the Thames and trying to drum the collision regulations into my head. This period of study was the only time in my life that I had spent any amount of time in London. As a group of young men I and my fellow students took full advantage of it. One of the boys had an old Humber staff car and on Sundays we would load up a keg of beer and drive out to the house of an old aunt who lived in Chertsey, to drink the beer and play vicious croquet all day and play pontoon all night. I became a bit involved in playing rugby although I was not very good and enjoyed most the drinking of beer with the team at the Cheshire Cheese on Fleet Street.

At about this time I became a cadet of the Honourable Company of Master Mariners. This organisation has its headquarters on HMS *Wellington* that is moored alongside the Embankment on the Thames. An important requirement of this appointment was that it insisted that the cadets kept a journal and had a mentor to encourage us in our careers. This was the start of my recording the events of my life throughout my long career. Unfortunately perhaps it also developed writing in a rather factual style with little space for recording emotions and more personal matters. When I had obtained my master's ticket in 1958 I became a member of the Honourable Company but resigned later. I was then in Canada and because my ongoing membership appeared not to offer me much value at that time in my career as I was unable to attend its regular technical meetings and I did not have a high opinion of its journal.

After obtaining the certificate for second mate I was required to get a further year and a half of sea time before the first mate study and exam. I decided to study for the next ticket and to go to the School of Navigation at Warsash on the Hamble River, near Southampton. I hoped that I would be able to compress my studies and to spend a bit less time on them. I have few social memories of that time except of drinking too much in local pubs and then trying to drive an old motor cycle, with about four of us riding it, around a local playing field after the pubs closed. We also rowed out to the school's sail training ship *Moyana* one night and stole the ceremonial cannons and hoisted them to the top of one of the school buildings! This was followed by the usual lectures and threats to punish all the offenders.

A significant occurrence during my time at Warsash was to meet John Morley, who had shared my time on the *Conway*. He told me that he was off to the Antarctic on the *John Biscoe* and that there were places for officers on another ship being modified for the Falkland Island Dependencies Survey (FIDS), called the *Shackleton*. This sounded much more exciting than becoming a Blue Funnel Captain. I do not think that at the time I had thoroughly thought about the implications of such a move. I would be sailing on smaller ships and the navigation would be more difficult. I was even going to be on ships that flew another flag, the Falkland Island ensign but it was likely to be much more thrilling than spending year after year on the Blue Funnel railway tracks to the Far East and back. It so happened that the large company of Alfred Holt and Co eventually went out of business due to its inability to diversify to meet changes in the business and shipping technology. However the Falkland Island Dependencies survey also changed in the years after I left with the signing of the Antarctic Treaty, the Falklands War and a change in name of the organisation to the British Antarctic Survey (BAS). All these changes were yet to happen when I was faced with the decision of remaining in the Blue Funnel Line or applying to the Crown Agents for the Colonies to join the Falkland Island fleet.

Happenings at Home

During my years with the Blue Funnel line I returned to Lamorna between voyages. My father was busy writing a series of books for boys about a Breton Crabber *Dauntless*. My mother worked on her art when she could find time from looking after the household. She was a good artist and had some of her works shown at the Royal Academy. I was much saddened in 1955 when my grandfather, by then a famous artist, died and I was called home from Bremen, where my current ship was berthed. My parents now inherited Flagstaff Cottage at Lamorna and continued to get on with their own careers of artist and author. My childhood friends had grown up and were scattered in distant parts of the World. My closest friend, Tim Evans, had moved to Wales, where he worked as an agricultural advisor. Others had gone to Southern Rhodesia and to Canada. Only Keith Gardiner, my closest neighbour, had remained in Lamorna to work as a diver. In spite of my professional career I had maintained a strong interest in recreational boating and over a period of years had a series of small sailing boats that I kept and sailed locally. For a time I sailed competitively in a locally designed boat called a *West of England Redwing* but was never a strong competitor and came near the back in most races. I became involved in local mackerel fishing, which at the time was booming and there were about six boats working commercially out of Lamorna. When I was at home the routine during the summer months was to go out fishing at four in the morning and fish until seven when we would join the local fishermen to pack the fish in boxes, load them in an old car and drive them to the Newlyn market. In the evenings the local fishing fleet would go out again at around six and fish until dark at ten. My mentor and advisor in this activity was a very tough local farm labourer called Jack Small, who fished every morning and evening and in addition worked on a nearby farm throughout the day. The local fishermen fished with gear called 'the feathers'. This was a clear nylon line with differently coloured feathers on thirty or so hooks. When the mackerel struck in shoals every one of the hooks would hold a leaping shimmering fish which were quickly removed from the line so that the feathers could be returned to the sea while the shoal was still around. Later developments of the fishing method involved having the line on a small drum, called a gurdy, that would be quickly lowered and raised and the fish forced off as the line passed an aperture. In the early days no gloves were worn and one was constantly pricked by the hooks and if you were unlucky the barb would pass through a soft piece of skin.

During my late teens and early twenties I had a girl friend called Yvonne Tancock whose family lived in St Ives. She was very happy to share my passion for sailing and the sea but was also a keen horse rider. She helped race the *Redwing* and was also happy to go out fishing with me. It was an idyllic time and we would sail up and down the coast of Mount's Bay and land on beautiful beaches at places such as Pedn Vounder to swim and picnic. During my study period at Warsash, Yvonne had a job looking after the ponies of the Devon and Somerset Staghounds and I became a camp follower. She was based at the stables in Exford, a pretty little Exmoor village. When I could get away from Warsash I would drive to Exford and camp. It was a lovely summer but it got very cold in the early mornings in my tent by the river and the stud groom and his wife took pity on me inviting me to be their guest with my main payment being to muck out the stables and to help exercise the ponies. On hunt days the stable girls would ride a second horse out for the huntsmen and I would follow the hunt on foot. In the evenings we would sometimes go out in the countryside to hear the stags baying. The expectation was that we would get married but my Antarctic ventures did not fit well with marriage. She went on to marry a farmer.

ANTARCTIC YEARS

The *Shackleton*

In 1954, following the advice of my *Conway* colleague John Morley I applied to the Crown Agents for the Colonies, which administered the ships of the Falkland Island Dependencies Survey (FIDS), for the job of Second Officer on the *Shackleton.* To my great pleasure I was summoned for an interview in London and was appointed to the job. The ship had previously been a small cargo passenger ship called *Arendal* that plied the Norwegian coast. The Falkland Island Government had bought it and was having it converted to an Antarctic Research ship at the fishing port of Frederikshavn in northern Denmark. The crew was assembled and sent to Denmark to collect the ship during a very cold November. We were housed in a little hotel during the final conversion of the ship. The hotel was rather basic and the landlady filled the bath with her pot plants and sent her guests down to the local bath house. During that time I got to know some of my future companions. Our Captain, Bill Johnston, was as far removed from the Blue Funnel captains with whom I had previously sailed as can be imagined. Bill was warm and friendly and supervised the refit and the eventual running of the ship with a minimum fuss. This was quite different from the distant management and supervision of the Blue Funnel Masters, who kept a good distance from their officers and crew and who I seldom met socially. I also met Tom Woodfield, who was to be the third officer and become a long term friend. He had also been in cargo passenger liners and had followed a career similar to my own. Later he was to become the Master of the Antarctic ships himself and eventually an Elder Brother of Trinity House, the lighthouse authority

Shackleton sailed for Southampton on a cold and stormy December day. At that time there were still mines left over from the war in the North Sea and ships had to follow swept channels between the mined areas. Unfortunately the storm was so great that the little ship had difficulty steering along those channels and probably wandered over several areas where mines might have existed. Another problem was a poorly installed oil cooking stove that allowed the most noxious fumes to escape and invade most of the ship. The result of that and the generally rough sea was that most of the crew were badly seasick. However the ship reached Southampton in early December and started to load the huge variety of materials that were needed to support the British Antarctic base camps. These included pre-fabricated houses, tractors, small boats and all manner of food and clothing. In between the work of loading there was a naming ceremony to call the ship after the famous Antarctic explorer Shackleton. Like all the Falkland Island Dependencies research ships it was designated a Royal Research Ship (RRS) but in fact was more a base support ship than a research ship. The ship was named by the wife of the Governor of the Falklands Mrs Elizabeth Arthur and a number of old explorers who had been with the expeditions Captain Scott attended the ceremony.

Christmas Card in Colour

R.R.S. "SHACKLETON" IN THE ANTARCTIC

For the first time, the Seafarers' Education Service has produced a Christmas Card in full colour, size as illustrated. The painting was a prizewinner in the S.E.S. competitions and is the work of Mr. A. J. Kerr, who was the *Shackleton's* second officer.

7/6 PER DOZEN *Post-free*

Complete with envelopes

Profits from the sale of the card, which contains no advertising matter, are devoted to the College of the Sea Endowment Fund. Orders should be sent to: The Secretary, Seafarers' Education Service, Mansbridge House, 207 Balham High Road, London, S.W.17.

Figure 8 Adam Kerr's watercolour of RRS *Shackleton* won a prize in the SES Competition, c1956.

The ship had been scheduled to sail before Christmas 1954 but as the last cargo was being loaded it was noted that every time the crane swung back and forth across the ship it rolled. Clearly the vessel was unstable and unseaworthy to meet the voyage and the task ahead. This was of particular concern when about to face the huge seas of the Southern Ocean. It was decided that the remedy was to ballast the bottom of the ship with pig iron. This meant unloading half the cargo before the ballast could be lowered and placed in the bottom of the ship. There was no time to get this work done before Christmas and the stevedores would be on holiday over the holidays. So the ship was to be in Southampton for Christmas. As we had already said our farewells to relatives and friends several of the crew decided not to go home but to stand by the ship. It was a jolly time with much partying. An invitation went out to invite the nurses from a local hospital to the ship. Tom Woodfield and I stayed on the ship as well as Bill Johnston, our Irish skipper, who showed that he could dance and drink with the best of them.

The loading of the ballast and re-loading of the cargo was completed and just before New Year's Day the ship sailed for Montevideo. I soon found that life aboard *Shackleton* was a lot more congenial than aboard a Blue Funnel liner. The officers were all assigned responsibilities and trusted in carrying them out. As Second Mate I was responsible for the navigation. Unlike the noon ceremony involving all the officers observing the sun's altitude to obtain the latitude I would take the noon sights myself and report any modification of course needed to the Captain over a gin and tonic in the wardroom. Of course all the deck officers had their own watch keeping and navigation responsibilities but there was not the continual irritating overseeing process of the Blue Funnel line. Tom Woodfield, the third mate and I got on well but we found the mate rather stiff. Nevertheless the deck officers all worked well as a team under the Captain. Besides the crew about twenty scientists and others on their way to spend time on the British Antarctic bases were carried aboard. They were expected to help the crew with the maintenance of the ship. Montevideo was a great stopover. It was a place where a few remaining base personnel could join the ship and some last minute cargo loaded. Lovely girls from Argentina were visiting Uruguay on holiday and helped the crew to idle away the nights ashore. From Montevideo *Shackleton* headed due south to the Falkland Islands with an increasing amount of wind and rough sea. Late in January the islands came in sight and the ship entered Port Stanley to secure alongside the Government dock.

The other ship of the Falkland Island fleet *John Biscoe* was alongside, having already made one trip to the Antarctic and back that season. She was an old wooden boom defence vessel and was due to be retired the next year. The ship was later sold to the New Zealand navy and a replacement built for the Falkland's Government. The Falkland Islands at that time was an old fashioned colony. The Governor lived in style at Government House and officers from visiting ships were expected to go and sign the Visitors' Book on arrival.

The Island economy was mainly driven by the Falkland Island Company. At that time sheep farming was the only serious source of commercial activity and there were sheep stations on most of the islands. Although there was an abundance of fish in the waters around the islands, particularly mullet, these were not fished commercially and offshore oil possibilities had yet to be considered.

A small ship the *Fitzroy* provided the only international transport for cargo and passengers between the islands and Montevideo.

Figure 9 RMS *Fitzroy* (Photo F Wooden).

There were at that time no international flights, although small aircraft were beginning to be used for transportation between Port Stanley and the scattered sheep stations. Most travel across the islands was by horse. There was no tourism although strangers who did visit the islands would be taken to see the colonies of gentoo and other small penguins. When riding across the islands between the sheep stations there were recognised 'gates', which were in reality just stopping places that were marked by piles of empty rum bottles.

Life for the ship's officers while in Port Stanley was very social. We were entertained by the local population but there were also exchange visits between the visiting ships which took the form of invitations aboard for film shows and drinks. The *Great Britain* that has now been transported to Bristol as a museum was at one time anchored in Port Stanley harbour but during a gale broke its anchor cable and drifted on to the rocks just outside the entrance to the harbour. For parties the ship's launch would visit the *Great Britain* to collect the mussels that grew in profusion on its sides. An annual event was the Sailors' Race in which crews from visiting ships would mount horses and race in a relay with a dummy in front of the saddle, which had to be passed to another rider at the end of each section of the course. Most of the sailors had little experience of riding horses and they were often the worse for wear from indulging in the rum that was imported to the colony in large quantities. Riding horses was also a way of entertaining the local ladies. One Sunday I borrowed two horses for a ride into the country but my companion's horse got trapped in one of the many quagmires on the islands. As the horse slowly sank in the mud the hysterical lady pulled off saddle and saddle blanket to provide it with some footing. Fortunately some men digging peat nearby brought their lorry over and hauled the horse onto dry land.

At that time, in the mid nineteen fifties, the Falkland Island Dependencies Survey (FIDS) occupied fourteen bases in Antarctica, all located on the Antarctic Peninsula, that long mountainous finger that reaches northwards towards South America. Some of the bases were located on islands off the peninsular, such as Admiralty Bay on the South Shetland Islands and on Signy Island on the South Orkney Islands. There was also a resident magistrate at Grytviken on South Georgia.

It was the task of the two ships *John Biscoe* and *Shackleton* to re-supply the bases with food and other material and to replace the personnel. These scientists typically spent two years on these isolated stations. Their skills ranged from surveying to medicine. The underlying reason for the FIDS activities in the Antarctic was to support Britain's claim to sovereignty of a sector of the Antarctic. At the same time Chile and Argentina had overlapping claims for the same sector and also maintained base camps. During my time of visiting the Antarctic polite diplomatic sparring took place between the various national claimants. Each country's ships carried observers from the other competing countries but would take the opportunity to visit their bases and deliver a note protesting their presence in the territory. They in turn would deliver a counter protest. At the working level it was all friendly and harmonious.

One of the memorable events was to carry a young Argentine navy observer aboard the Shackleton for two weeks. He was charming and played the guitar with great skill. When it was time to deliver him to his own ship Shackleton went alongside his larger Argentine ship while at anchor in a place called Paradise Harbour. The officers were invited to a great dinner and the only note of disharmony was that the Argentine Captain would not step aboard Shackleton as she flew the Falkland Island ensign, which had a Union Jack incorporated in the hoist. The morning after the party when the British ship left the Argentine ship our Captain sailed Shackleton in circles around the other vessel with one of our scientists playing the bagpipes on the top

Figure 10 Falkland Islands Dependencies Stamps.

bridge! What a pity that some years later diplomacy broke down and Argentina invaded South Georgia and that led to the Falklands war. During the cruises the ships regularly carried important persons from the Falkland Government, including the Governor and the Bishop. During my second year the Duke of Edinburgh stopped at the Falklands during a World cruise of the Royal Yacht Britannia and then transferred to the new John Biscoe for a cruise along the Antarctic Peninsula.

The task of the base personnel was essentially to show the flag. There were post offices at all the bases and these sold stamps, which had pictures of the ships of various historic expeditions.

Figure 11 Canso Flying Boat at Deception Island (Photograph F Wooden).

There was an active programme of surveying and mapping of the topography, geology and various biological studies of the penguins and other animals. During my two years in the area a major aerial survey was carried out by a Canadian company, Hunting Surveys. Their two aircraft, Canso flying boats, were based on Deception Island.

The results of this work which for the first time mapped the entire coastline of the peninsular in detail, was a major advance in the exploration. Mapping on land by the methods employed to that date was a slow and difficult task as the area is extremely mountainous with huge glaciers and ice falls tumbling into the sea. Although some small tracked vehicles were being used around the bases all the long distance travel was undertaken by dog sleigh. The presence of dogs, no longer allowed in the Antarctic, posed many logistical problems. Until then the animals had to be

Figure 12 Adam Kerr, Salveson's whale catcher, watercolour.

acquired in Greenland, Canada and other northern countries and shipped to the Antarctic. Once there the huskies had to be fed and this meant killing and providing seal meat. The killing of seals was a distasteful business as the half dead seals would frequently slide off the ice floes into the sea. The scientific personnel that we carried aboard were very unhappy with the seal massacre but somehow food had to be obtained for the teams of huskies on which much of the field work depended. Visiting base camps from the relatively pristine environment of the ship the first thing one noticed was the pervasive smell of seal oil.

The trip across from Port Stanley to the first of the Antarctic bases to be reached, usually Admiralty Bay, on the South Shetland Islands was about 600 miles of often extremely rough ocean. During the summer months when I first visited the area the ice was quite broken up along the west coast of the Peninsula, this was fortunate because *Shackleton* was only lightly ice strengthened and not very powerful. One of the more interesting places visited was Deception Island, which was a large volcanic caldera that was still quite active. In front of the British base in Whaler Bay, the black sandy beach steamed from the volcanic extrusion. Further into the caldera there was an Argentine base.

One of the events during our visit was to see a whale catcher of the Salveson's fleet, fast aground on the rocks beside the narrow entrance to Port Foster. The whale catcher had entered the bay at full speed, made three tight circles and then crashed into the rocks on the way out!

Presumably the catcher was not a 'dry ship'. Our ship gradually worked its way south along the Danco Coast of Graham Land – the name given by the British to the peninsula. The coastline is remarkably scenic with high peaked mountains on the mainland side, between which icefalls plunge to the sea. Cape Renard on the northern end of the Lemaire Channel is the most scenic and much photographed peak. Horseshoe Island in Margarite Bay was the furthest southern point that we visited. The Captain tried to press south towards Alexandria Land, a large island at the base of the Antarctic Peninsula, but we encountered heavy pack ice and were obliged to return to the north.

Figure 13 Cape Renard, Lemaire Channel (Photo F Wooden).

At Port Lockroy, one of the bases visited, that is still active to this day, the Governor of the Falklands came aboard. He was a very keen skier and suggested that the young officers should accompany him ashore to try skiing. There were of course no lifts and for uphill travel seal skins provided the traction under the skis. Provided one avoided the crevasses this was a safe activity and my first introduction to a sport in which I greatly enjoyed in later years. Once more In early April the ship headed across the turbulent Drake Passage and arrived at Port Stanley on 8 April. Aboard was a happy crowd of base personnel on their way home. A brief time was spent in the Falklands before heading once more to Montevideo and home to Southampton on May 25 1957, just five days after my 24th birthday.

On return to Southampton the ship was taken to Thornycroft's shipyard where it would undergo a refit during the summer. The officers were to share the task of representing the FIDS organisation while the refit was taking place and enjoy some leave. As we could not live on board the ship it was necessary to find some accommodation ashore. Tom Woodfield and I decided that we should buy a small yacht to live aboard on the Hamble River when we were standing by the ship and go off cruising together when the mate was standing by the ship.

Well Earned Leave

A South African sold us *Marishka*, a 27 foot gaff rigged cutter. It was venerable, having been built on the Clyde in 1896 but suitable for our purposes. The moorings on the Hamble River covered a much smaller area than those of today. During the long summer Tom and I had various exciting sails in our little boat, across the Channel and as far west as Land's End. There were of course some female company on some of these trips and a fair quantity of alcohol was consumed.

Figure 14 *Marishka* in Mount's Bay.

A particularly memorable voyage was not on *Marishka* but on a 35 foot Colin Archer designed boat that the South African had bought after selling us *Marishka* and planned to sail to South Africa. He invited me to help him sail the boat to Plymouth, where it was to be completely re-rigged. Unfortunately during the trip the yacht was caught in the middle of the English Channel by one of the classic storms that was later to be discussed by Adlard Coles in his book *Heavy Weather Sailing*. During the gale, besides having a malfunctioning engine most of the halyards were lost up the mast and at one time we were rolled on our side to an extent that I thought my last hour had come. However the eye of the storm passed by and a start up the Channel was made with a very small sail set and towing fenders behind as a sea anchor. In this condition an offer of a tow by a naval frigate was made, which was reluctantly accepted by my skipper, especially as they insisted that they passed a steel towing wire. During this process the frigate managed, through poor seamanship, to get the tow wire around its propeller. The yacht was cast adrift, leaving the naval vessel with the two black balls of the not under command signal flying and a request to call the lifeboat. This eventually arrived and towed the South African's yacht, in a bedraggled state, into Portsmouth

One further incident marked that summer. During the previous season in the Antarctic the *Shackleton's* officers had started some very amateur hydrographic surveying because the navigational charts of the Antarctic were extremely poor. The UK Hydrographic Office, recognising these efforts, arranged for the three *Shackleton* officers to spend two weeks taking a course on hydrography at the naval base at Chatham. The instructor, who I was to get to know very well in later years, was Lieutenant Commander David Haslam. He was a congenial man and much was learnt from him during our short course. The students also had great fun socialising with their instructor. One day while we were having a drink together in the wardroom David Haslam recounted how he had been out on HMS *Dryad*, the navy's navigational training ship, giving the trainees some points on hydrography. He told us how he had never been so ashamed of the navy in his life when the *Dryad* had gone to take a yacht in tow during the recent epic storm. He then told the story of how his ship had attempted to tow the South African's yacht and what a mess had been made. That coincidence was the start of a long life time friendship and eventually a working relationship between David Haslam and myself, which will be related later in this book.

Second Year in the Antarctic

The second voyage to the Antarctic set sail much earlier in the year to take advantage of the full summer season. On 1 October 1955 the ship was ready to depart. A group of dignitaries met on the quay at Southampton to see the ship on its way. These included Sir Raymond Priestly, who had been on the Scott expedition and Dr Vivian Fuchs, who then headed the FIDS office. The voyage out stopped at more ports than on the previous year including the Canary Islands and Recife in Brazil, besides once more stopping in Montevideo. Two weeks were spent in Port Stanley with the usual busy social time, before heading off for South Georgia. There the ship called first at Leith Harbour, the base for the Salveson's whaling operations and then at Grytviken, where another whaling station, Argentine de Pescas was established.

Figure 15 Flensing whales at Grytviken.

Both of these shore stations were in full operation with the whales being flensed and tried – a bloody and smelly operation. The huge carcases were pulled up on a slipway where the blubber was cut from end to end with flensing knives and then pulled back like peeling a banana. The huge strips of blubber were then cut into pieces and fed to the try pots to be rendered down into whale oil. Grytviken was the home of the British magistrate and also the site of the grave of the famous explorer Shackleton. Later in the season we carried 500 live sheep from Rincon Grande on the Falklands to Leith Harbour as food for the whalers. With a great deal of difficulty we herded the sheep into our wooden barge and ferried them out to the ship. Once aboard and down in the hold they were packed tight so that they would not be knocked over and trampled to death by the other sheep. They were happy to reach the dry land of South Georgia.

Figure 16 Building a cairn for Porquoi Pas, Peterman Island (Photo F Ryan).

The trip to South Georgia was the start of an active programme, returning to Port Stanley for a period over Christmas before going to the Antarctic once more. Rather than list the many bases visited just some of the more memorable events will be discussed. On Peterman Island near the Argentine Islands Base a cairn had to be erected to commemorate the voyage of a French expedition ship called *Pourquoi Pas.* The base personnel had found a sheet of lead with the names of all the members of that expedition inscribed on it and thought it would be appreciated if it was returned to Paris. This was not the case as it provided evidence that the French expedition had been there and the French Government asked that the plaque be returned. The British Foreign Office arranged for the lead sheet with all Porquoi Pas' crew names engraved be suitably mounted on an oak base and this was to be mounted on a large cairn. This was done and sits on Peterman Island to this day as a memorial to the early exploration of the French.

Another memorable event was a medical operation carried out at sea somewhere between the Falklands and the Antarctic Peninsula. Aboard the ship, on his way to be deployed on an Antarctic base, we carried a young Scottish doctor. He was newly qualified and anxious to try his hand at what he had learned at medical school. Fortunately for him one

Figure 17 Adam Kerr on deck off Signy Island.

of the engine room crew developed appendicitis. The doctor believed that an operation was needed and the Captain took the ship into the quiet shelter of a large tabular iceberg. A sheet was spread on the wardroom table and the ship's officers were given various tasks. The doctor was to carry out the surgery while our German dentist was to be the assistant surgeon. In fact he was a keen photographer and spent most of his time jumping up on chairs and photographing the operation. The third mate was the pentathol pusher. A needle full of the drug was inserted and strapped to the patient's arm and on a signal from the doctor he was to push the plunger by small amounts. I was involved in another anaesthetic procedure of dripping ether on a mask over the patients face. After a certain amount of fumbling around the appendix was found and removed from which the patient fortunately recovered. The medical authorities in Port Stanley were not overly impressed by the operation as it was felt that the appendicitis could have been kept quiet with penicillin while the ship returned to the more sterile environment of the hospital in Port Stanley. This operation was rather less daunting than the removal of an eye from a geologist on another expedition in Antarctica several years before. In that case there were no qualified medical practitioners and the whole operation was carried out under instructions over a radio.

During the second season the officers were able to follow the lessons they had learnt on hydrographic surveying. The ship's motor launch had been equipped with an echo sounder and rather heavy Troughton & Sims theodolites were provided with which to measure the triangulation. At that time there were no satellites and no electronic way of positioning and so horizontal sextant angles provided the main means of positioning the soundings.

Figure 18 Skuas were prolific and a constant danger to all other birds.

An area around Danco Island was a main target of the surveys for a site for a future base that was, in fact, never built, My own name of Kerr was officially applied to a headland in the survey area. The Falkland Island ships were not the only ones carrying out hydrographic surveys in the area because the British navy had HMS *Protector*, a large vessel working in the area that was equipped with helicopters and had a separate survey party. It is probable that the surveys that we delivered to the Admiralty Hydrographic Office at the end of the season were much less professional than theirs!

Before leaving the Antarctic some words must be said about the teaming wild life that was always to be seen. On the trips across the Southern Ocean many kinds of albatross were always to be observed gracefully gliding across the waves and following the ship. At the other end of the scale were the little Wilson stormy petrels, dancing across the waves as they gently picked up krill and other small organisms from the sea surface. Various other kinds of petrel, including pintado or cape pigeons and white chinned petrels were frequently seen. Skuas were prolific and a

Figure 19 Chinstrap Penguins.

constant danger to all other birds, particularly the young penguins. Various kinds of seals, including elephant seals were present on many of the beaches we visited. Care had to be taken to avoid the aggressive leopard seals. The smaller penguins had their colonies everywhere, with chinstrap and gentoo penguins being the most prolific. The larger emperor and king penguins were not generally seen on the Antarctic Peninsula as their colonies were further south.

On 18 May 1956 *Shackleton's* work was finished in the Southern Hemisphere. A brief stop was made at Port Stanley. During that visit I met a returning member of the FIDS crews, who had spent two years in one of the bases. This was Wally Herbert, who later in life became a great explorer and was a most talented painter and photographer. He made epic journeys to both Poles and was knighted for his adventures[7]. I was inspired by his work and planned to arrange a show of my own art, mainly water colours of penguins, the following year when we visited Port Stanley Due to a future turn of events I did not return to Port Stanley but Tom Woodfield arranged a show of my work and some of my work probably still graces the walls of my Falkland Island friends. The ship set sail for Southampton via Montevideo and Recife. Arriving on 5 June another annual refit began in Thornycroft's yard. The same routine as before was resumed, with Tom Woodfield and I living aboard our yacht *Marish*ka on the Hamble River when we were standing by the ship and going

---

[7] Sir Wally Herbert, *The Polar World – the Unique Vision of Sir Wally Herbert*, Polar World, 2007.

off cruising together when we were both free.

My plans to spend another season on *Shackleton* going to the Antarctic were interrupted by events at home. My father had a commission to write a biography about the doctor-missionary Wilfred Grenfell[8] who had done wonders in improving the condition of the fishermen on the coast of Labrador and Newfoundland. At that time I was very fired up about polar exploration and thought it might be interesting to see the Arctic. I asked my father to keep his eye open for any job opportunities that would take me to the Arctic. It so happened, that flying somewhere in eastern Canada, he sat next to a man who was carrying a sextant. This led to the information that the Canadian Government was recruiting masters and mates to be trained as hydrographic surveyors. He came home with this information and I applied to Ottawa and received the news that I had won a competition – whatever a competition might be! I now had to extract myself from the work with the Falkland Island Government and make arrangements to go to Canada. At the time I never thought that it would lead to spending nearly thirty years of my life in that country. The Crown Agents fortunately found a replacement third mate for *Shackleton*. Tom Woodfield was promoted into the position of second officer and was later to become a senior master with the FIDS vessels. Before I took on my new job in Canada my father had suggested that I should complete my exams for master

[8] J Lennox Kerr, *Wilfred Grenfell, his Life and Work*, George G Harrap, 1959.

mariner. I was three months short of the sea time required and while I could have completed the time by staying with the *Shackleton* I thought it would be more expeditious to complete the time on other British ships.

CHANGING TACK

The *Tortuguero*

In order to obtain the required sea time for my Master's certificate after leaving the *Shackleton* I first decided to join a ship of the General Steam Navigation Company, the *Gronigen* on some trips in European waters but found this did not count for the full sea time of deep water ships. So I looked elsewhere and ended up on a ship called the *Tortuguero,* owned by Elders and Fyffes, which transported bananas. The ships were smart, white painted and traded to West Africa and the West Indies. The business was new to me. Bananas are carried at a constant temperature of 52 degrees Fahrenheit. They arrive on board in green bunches and only ripen when brought ashore at the end of the voyage. They are stowed in small compartments to prevent them being crushed. Once the cargo is loaded It was a job of the officers to take the temperatures twice a day. That involves climbing through numerous hatches and along the different decks by torch light and reading all the thermometers. Today this operation will be carried out by some remote reading system. Just before my first trip the *London Illustrated News* published an article concerning all the insects and occasionally snakes that were sometimes carried aboard with the bananas. As you lifted a hatch to climb to the next deck above it was possible that a tarantula or similar nasty creature might drop down on you. Fortunately this did not happen while I was aboard apart from finding a very sleepy tarantula that was completely numbed by the cold.

Figure 20 Adam Kerr, SS *Tortuguero*, watercolour.

Two trips were made on the *Tortuguero* for me to complete the required sea time. On each occasion the ship went to what was then the British Cameroons stopping at a port up a muddy river at a place called Tiko. Bananas were also loaded at Sta Isabel on Fernando Po, a Spanish Island off the African coast. After the two trips I arrived at Garston Dock in Liverpool with all the sea time necessary to sit my master's ticket on January 13 1958. With my eventual departure to Canada for an unknown period of time I decided that I would study at Plymouth, which was close to my home in Cornwall.

Certificate of Crossing the Line.

By Royal Decree.

Whereas; Be it known to one and all that on the: .....15th day of [illegible]...in the Year of Grace [illegible] one...............did presnet himself for the purpose of paying forfeit due to trespass.

This is to certify that the person herein, before specified has met his obligations, and was duly shaved bathed and induced to take a pill. He now has the freedom of the Seven Seas, and may pass the Equator without let or hindrance, at any time during the day or night.

This certificate is not transferable, and must not be sold or otherwise disposed of.

No mortages can be raised upon it, nor can it be taken to pawn.

Witnessed by my Hand and Seal this day.

Witnesses: [illegible] Neptunus Rex: [illegible]

Figure 21 Adam Kerr, Crossing the Line Certificate, watercolour.

It was a cold winter and my lodgings were chilly and the food poor. However I was determined to get the studying done quickly. While my studies for my mate's ticket had taken four weeks, I had to allocate seven weeks for my masters and although the written exams were passed with no problem I managed to fail the oral exam by the mistake of sailing the model down the wrong side of a line of wreck marking buoys. Although the studying was in Plymouth the exams were taken in Cardiff. This now presented a dilemma. Passage to Canada was already booked but I had to re-sit the oral exam. Fortunately this was successfully passed and I was able to pack for Canada. I could now sign up for my new job with a master mariner's certificate in my hand.

WORKING FOR THE CANADIAN HYDROGRAPHIC SERVICE

First Impressions of Canada

I had planned to sail to Canada on the Cunard ship *Ivernia*. My father had encouraged me to travel in second class as he said that I would have more fun but I decided that as I was going as a passenger, for once in my life I should get a first class ticket. As it happened, although first class passengers were not supposed to go into other class accommodation, I had a great amount of freedom and saw the first of my new country early one morning from the porthole of the cabin of a young diplomat's wife. The ship stopped at Quebec City on the way up the St Lawrence River to put some of the French Canadian passengers ashore. I remembered being rather surprised that they spoke French! Such was an Anglophile education! I was to learn a lot more about that division of Canadian society over the years.

First memories are always vivid and I recall Montreal for its hot streets dusty streets and huge cars. I also remembered the train journey to Ottawa in a most comfortable carriage. This was a continuation of my first class ticket and I sat in a large swivel chair. There were only about a dozen chairs in the compartment and the passengers were waited on by an attendant. Arriving at Ottawa's large Union Station in the centre of the city my father had suggested that I stay at a hotel with a Scottish name, which proved to be the Lord Elgin Hotel. I had arrived at Montreal on May 17 1958, just two days short of my twenty-fifth birthday. This is Victoria Day and is a long weekend holiday in Canada and the city was very deserted. I had been given the names of Graham and Diana Rowley by my father. Both had strong contacts with Polar exploration. They very kindly invited me to their place in Rockliffe, one of the well to do suburbs of the city. Graham, who had a senior position in the Government, was soon in contact with the Dominion Hydrographer, FCG Smith, finding out what opportunities there would be for me to go to the Arctic. Later, through him, I was put in contact with many of the old Canadian Arctic hands.

Reporting for Duty

With the long weekend over I reported to the offices of the Canadian Hydrographic Service. These were in some temporary buildings, which were the vestiges of war but had remained standing into a period of peace. I was interviewed by Steve Titus, a giant of a man, who was in charge of all the survey operations. Like many of the older surveyors he was a civil engineer. It was in fact the difficulty of the service to attract civil engineers that had made the Canadian Government look overseas and try to attract masters and mates in the United Kingdom. I was told that I was assigned to go on a chartered sealing ship, the *Algerine,* to work on surveys in the Sub Arctic but first of all, waiting for the ice to clear, to go to Newfoundland. I was introduced to the rest of the surveyors that were going on *Algerine* and other survey ships. A number of the surveyors were expatriates with qualifications as masters and mates. As survey ships did not leave Nova Scotia until the ice had cleared in the Belle Isle Strait between Newfoundland and the Labrador, I was first to be sent with a fellow surveyor, Ken Williams, to Barrington Passage in southwest Nova Scotia. This entailed a long train journey to Halifax and then a change of trains to take us south westwards through Nova Scotia. Canadian trains on these long journeys provided a choice of comfortable accommodation. You could choose to share a cabin with your friends or be by yourself in an ingenious little compartment called a roomette, which included your bed, table, toilet and everything needed for your comfort. Intriguing was a locker in which you put your shoes, to recover them in the morning beautifully polished overnight by the attendant.

Barrington Passage is near a busy fishing port called Clark's Harbour and the survey had a base in the harbour and several survey launches berthed alongside. I was quartered in a private house about a mile away. The purpose of the survey was to establish the geographic coordinates of points along the coast, which would later be used to position survey boats and ships over the adjacent sea. The survey was using a newly invented South African electronic device called a Tellurometer, which measured distances very precisely between points that were several miles apart. The measurement of these distances and the angles between the sections measured by theodolite constituted a survey traverse. However the first requirement was to build wooden towers that were between 30 and 40 feet high. The instruments were mounted on these towers so that lines of sight over the dense spruce tree coverage could be obtained for each leg of the traverse. The construction of these towers was a form of engineering in itself. First large quantities of timber, nails and tools for the construction had to be assembled at the site. As most of the sites were located on offshore islands all these materials had to be transported by boat and then carried on the shoulders of the survey team to the location. At that time of year, in late May, the weather warms up rapidly and there is much fog. As the survey launch motored out to the offshore islands the boat would be steered carefully through the fog avoiding the numerous lobster fishing boats that would appear out of the gloom. Clark's Harbour is a very active centre for lobster fishing and the nearby waters contain a mass of gaily painted buoys marking the location of the traps. Arriving at the islands the crew would get all the material ashore and hike up to the site with the timber or lumber as Canadians call it, on their shoulders. A site would often have to be cleared before the construction could start. The plan was to build two tripod towers, one inside the other. The objective was for the instruments to be placed at the apex of the inner tripod and the surveyors would stand on the external tripod. In that way the delicate instruments would not be disturbed by the surveyor as he moved around the instrument taking his measurements. The method of construction was to make one side of the inner tripod lying on the ground and then erect it using a block and tackle secured to a convenient tree and inserting the third leg, so that all three legs formed a triangle on the ground. The outer tower was constructed in the same manner. The towers were mainly made from cut 3" by 4" milled wood but in some of the more remote sites they would be constructed of spruce trees cut at the site. The final task was to place a brass survey monument (plug) in the ground immediately beneath the apex of the tower to precisely mark the geographic spot. During the lunch breaks, by which time the hot sun had burnt off the fog, the surveyors and crew would sit around eating out of their lunch pails while enjoying the sweet smell of spruce trees. The lunch pails seemed to be very much a North American invention with sandwiches and thermos of tea or coffee stored neatly in a metal container.

Returning to the base the surveyors would then go off to their lodgings. Surveyors are notoriously heavy drinkers and also sharing the lodging house was one of our crew who had been imbibing enthusiastically the night before. During breakfast we were discussing the persistent fog and he had verbally attacked me. 'What's the matter with you f.....g English.? Don't you get bad weather over there?' Up to that time I had found my Canadian colleagues most friendly but this outburst set me back, although later I realised that this was not normal behaviour. Of an evening I would go down to a bridge over a nearby river where a herring like fish called gaspereaux were running up to spawn. The locals were assigned certain strategic points, where they would stand on rocks with large dip nets to catch the fish running up the river. On weekends I would take advantage of the trout fishing in the nearby brooks and rivers. Brook trout abounded but making ones way along the rivers was difficult as the dense spruce forest grew right to the river banks. There was excellent salmon fishing in nearby rivers, such as the Le Have but without a car these were not accessible to me. After spending two weeks in Barrington Passage and being introduced to my new job, it was time to join my ship, which was in Pictou on the northern coast of Nova Scotia.

Pictou was a field base of the organisation and several of the survey ships were berthed alongside the dock preparing for their summer season. *Algerine* and another chartered sealing vessel, the *North Star* were alongside and a venerable Government survey ship called *Acadia*. During the days there was much for the surveyors to do in checking, calibrating and loading their equipment. The surveyors were quartered ashore in an hotel. For recreation the crews drank in the Canadian Legion and the surveyors in an anachronistic establishment, called the Gentlemen's Club. The mainstays of the town's society such as the doctor and editor of the local newspaper drank there regularly. During this time in Pictou I got to know some of the surveyors from the other ships. One of these was Mike Eaton, an ex-UK naval surveyor. We got on well and later worked and socialised together.

The day came for departure in early June 1958. The ship headed across the Gulf of St Lawrence to the extreme north of Newfoundland, to a remote fishing village called Quirpon. This faced out on the Belle Isle Straits that separated Newfoundland from the coast of Labrador. The survey party was to spend a month there while it waited for the ice to clear further north up the coast of Labrador. The Belle Isle Straits provide an important sea route during the summer months for ships on their way from Europe to the St Lawrence River and the heart of Canada. Large ice bergs floating down from the north, provide a hazard for the passing ships but during the summer the pack ice, which prevents all shipping movement in the winter, clears away and passage through the Straits greatly shortens the route from Europe into Canada and Great Lakes ports of the USA. In the middle of the strait the isolated rock and lighthouse of Belle Isle provides an important navigational beacon. Quirpon was a busy fishing village for the cod that were plentiful in those days but sadly have been over fished and the stock practically decimated. During the surveys the crews would step ashore on the shingly beaches and wade through a spongy mass of roe from the capelin, a small fish that was a main diet for the cod. In the water just outside the band of roe the capelin would be swimming around and it was possible to dip quantities out in buckets. The local people would catch the capelin and dry them on racks in the sun to provide winter food for themselves and their dogs. During respites from the surveys it was possible to stop and throw a cod jigger over the side and with no effort catch large cod. The jigger is a simple lead weight of about half a kilo with two huge hooks that was tied to a piece of cod line. This method was used in the dories fishing offshore from the large schooners, as was described in the book *Captains Courageous* by Rudyard Kipling. Local fishermen used that method but also had wooden fish traps up and down the coast. All the fish were delivered to the local plant to be gutted and split. Handling of the fish would not pass the standards of today as pitch forks were used to toss the cod from the boats onto the dock at the fish plant. The surveyors would go to the plant in the evenings to ask for the large cod heads to remove the tongues and cheeks, which when fried made delicious eating.

Figure 22 Survey Launch.

However, the party was not there to fish but to survey. *Algerine* carried two 30 foot survey launches which did most of the work. The first task was, as in Barrington Passage, to put in the geographic marks on shore. This was done by triangulating the marks along the coast. Wooden marks, that were painted white, were built along the shoreline. As there were no trees but only dense scrub, the carrying of the material to build the marks was hard work. Added to this the black flies and mosquitoes were ferocious. Although the surveyors would lather themselves with repellent this did not completely prevent the fierce attacks of the insects. An added difficulty was getting ashore on the rough coast. Materials and men were usually ferried from the survey launches to the shore in dories. On one of our first landings a dory capsized just offshore dipping its crew into the ice cold water! Fortunately all were picked up and survived. Following the work ashore the team started the surveys at sea. The launches were equipped with echo sounders, but at that time electronic positioning systems had not been introduced, and all positioning was by sextants that were used to simultaneously measure two horizontal angles between the marks we had established ashore. While the launches worked in the water close to the shore the ship itself worked offshore and in more comfortable conditions. On the launches two surveyors were continuously measuring pairs of angles and plotting them with a device called a station pointer, to position the boat. This was difficult work when the sea was rough and the spray was flying – particularly for those who wore glasses. A coxswain, under the surveyor's instruction, kept the boat on the previously planned parallel course, perpendicular to the general line of the coast. At the end of each long day in the launches the surveyors would return to the mother ship. After a quick meal they would 'ink in' all the depth measurements on a master plot, called the 'field sheet.' The survey operation extended six days a week. On Saturday night a welcome bottle of rum was provided by the charterer. Sundays were a day of rest when many of the crew would go fishing for the brook trout that were prolific in the many small streams.

The *Algerine* then headed northwards towards Cape Chidley, the extreme north point of Labrador. The pack ice had cleared off the coast of Labrador but on rounding Cape Chidley and entering Ungava Bay the ship had to find its way through the floating pack ice. The destination was the Payne River on the west side of the Bay. An industrialist, Cyrus Eaton, planned to develop the large quantities of iron ore found in the area and the task was to survey the channel so that ships could export the material. In that part of Ungava Bay the tides are huge with a range of over 10 metres and the currents very strong. Payne River is quite remote, the only habitation on the river being a Hudson Bay post with its Scottish factor and his Inuit wife. Occasional wandering bands of Inuits would camp along the river and their white tents could be seen along the shoreline. The survey was to be carried out at a large scale and in view of the strong currents that rushed in and out of the river the first task was to survey the location of numerous stakes that would be planted along the shoreline and that would be used to provide steering marks for the launches. This resulted in the crew spending a lot of time along the foreshore and a chance to observe the plentiful wild life. Occasionally polar bears could be seen, to which a wide berth was given. Arctic foxes and hares were numerous and easy to see because they kept their white coats throughout the summer, even though the snow was no longer on the ground. The surveyors trying to shoot the hares for the pot discovered that if you whistled they would stop to listen, giving the hunter a chance to catch up with his prey. Ptarmigan, a type of grouse, kept most of their white feathers and were exceedingly tame. They could be easily knocked down by a thrown stone. Arctic char, magnificent fish similar to salmon, were prolific both in the main Payne River and in its many tributaries and nearby lakes. When the survey boats anchored for lunch we could cast a lure over the side and catch these fine fish with the greatest of ease. Typically they grew to about 5 kilograms weight.

The survey routine was much the same as it had been in Newfoundland. The working days were long and it was unusual to have Sundays off. One of the surveyors, Austin Quirk, was a skilled curry cook and once a week the crew enjoyed a fine curry made from what had been caught on the land, such as geese and hares and what could be found in the ship's stores. This would usually be washed down with the weekly quota of rum. After carrying out the basic survey task the area had to be swept to ensure that the surveyors had not failed to detect any hidden dangers. This consisted of drifting down the inlet with the current in a survey launch with an assembly of wires and floats that were designed to snag any obstacles on the sea floor. To date, as far as it is known, no large ship has ever entered the river and the clearance surveys have yet to be tested. Another final task was to measure the current velocity in the river. This was a difficult task as the launches had to be first anchored in the strong current. A paddle wheel instrument was then lowered over the side and its revolutions could be equated to the current speed. Measurements showed that there were currents as high as 8 knots. This was about the maximum speed of the survey launches and would have made navigation for a large ship extremely difficult.

Figure 23 A Peterhead in the Payne River.

About once a month a Peterhead, a type of Scottish fishing boat would arrive from Leaf Bay, a settlement some distance to the south. It brought the all important mail and some fresh supplies. Occasionally a Government icebreaker would visit Payne River but during the summer months there was no ice to break and its main task was to carry vital supplies to the settlement, although most of that work was done by the Hudson Bay Company's own ships.

For most of the summer the weather was remarkably good. The visibility in the clear Arctic air was excellent and the sun shone much of the time. Occasional storms would pass through making field work impossible but during those times it gave us a welcome respite to remain aboard and process the data. In mid September the weather quickly deteriorated and snow started to fall. The final field work of taking in the tide gauges and obtaining last details of the area were carried out and it was time to go south. *Algerine* reached Nova Scotia again in early October. During October and November the weather in Canada gets increasingly bitter and I was glad to be finally released to return to Ottawa. However an opportunity arose for me to join a survey party measuring distances by Tellurometer on the St Lawrence River between Kingston and Brockville. At Kingston we climbed to the top of a large grain elevator by means of a small conveyor belt called a 'humphry' from which we could see a long distance down the St Lawrence River. Working east from Kingston and down the St Lawrence River you pass through the scenic Thousand Islands, although at that time of year, in November, it is rather bleak with all the leaves off the trees and the many summer cottages closed up for the winter.

The Polar Continental Shelf Project (PCSP)

In Ottawa I established myself in some simple accommodation and I began life as an office worker. My friends were initially my survey acquaintances of whom

Austin Quirk, a fellow expatriate and his Scottish wife were my closest friends. I took up a Canadian way of life and watched the ice hockey on Saturday nights. I was introduced to the Arctic Circle group by Graham Rowley. Amongst these was a well known biologist Tom Manning. I stayed out in the bush in sub-zero weather while helping him build a log cabin. Tom and his friend Andrew MacPherson were old arctic hands and they were quite happy to be out in the bush in sub-zero weather. I also took up rugby again. Once more this was more for the social side than for my ability as a player. The Ottawa team was called the 'Bytown Beavers.' At that time the players were mostly expatriates and not very fit ones at that but the team soon started to recruit fitter and larger Canadians and over the years that trend carried Canadian rugby to a much higher standard than it had previously and eventually was to take it to an international level. One of the expatriates I got to know during that time was Peter Waddell, who led me to other contacts that were to have a large part to play in my life. I spent many of the weekends skiing with Mike Eaton at Camp Fortune, a ski resort not far from Ottawa in the Gatineau Hills. Through him I became aware that a major expedition called the Polar Continental Shelf Project was planned and that there were to be places for hydrographers. Mike had already requested an assignment and later I also applied to join.

In the late nineteen fifties a Government supported group of geologists called Operation Franklin, had discovered evidence of oil and gas in the Arctic Archipelago. Coal had already been found. The Canadian Government had also become concerned about its sovereignty over the Arctic Archipelago. The establishment of the Distant Early Warning Line – the DEW Line and other lines of defence in northern Canada had led to an increasing number of American citizens living and working in the area. Added to that there was some evidence that Soviet aircraft had been landing on the ice in the marine area over which Canada claimed sovereignty. All these matters caused the Canadian Government to plan a major scientific expedition, during which the systematic collection of geographic information would be organised. This was to be the Polar Continental Shelf Project and its field programme would be initially based at Isachsen on Ellef Ringnes Island at about 78 degrees North latitude. Dr Fred Roots, a Canadian geologist, who had great polar experience and had spent time in Antarctica as well as the Arctic was chosen as the first leader. I was not initially selected as one of the two hydrographers who were to participate in the expedition but Mike Eaton broke his leg in a skiing accident and I was asked to join as a replacement.

The best time to start field work in that part of the Arctic is in early March. There is at that time an increasing amount of daylight although the temperatures are still very cold at typically around - 40 degrees Celsius. A group of us left Ottawa on March 9 1959 and travelled by Royal Canadian Air Force (RCAF) plane to Churchill and then on to Resolute. At that time the facilities in that settlement were mainly limited to those supporting the RCAF. There was a small Inuit community some distance away. Resolute is now an important Arctic hub and is serviced by commercial airlines.

From Resolute men and materials were transported by the expedition's own chartered aircraft, which were initially a single engine Otter and a Beaver chartered from McMurray Airlines in Uranium City. Larger aircraft in the form of a Bristol freighter and an Avro York were chartered to move the heavier supplies.

Isachsen, on Ellef Ringnes Island, a further several hundred miles to the north was to be our base. That remote spot was the site of a joint Canada-USA meteorological station and became headquarters for the PCSP party. The buildings in which the group lived were made of wood but well insulated. With a permanent cook there was no shortage of good food. However the extreme cold ruled everything. A memory of just how cold it was, was the forty five gallon barrel that was placed between the sleeping and eating buildings in which you stopped to pee as you passed. When it was full of solidly frozen urine we would simply roll it away down the hill to be forgotten in some remote gully. Today of course such practice would be condemned but in those early days we had much less concern for the environment. If aircraft closed down their engines they could not be re-started without the use of a Herman Nelson heater. Lead acid batteries did not operate at all well in such temperatures and nickel cadmium batteries were required to operate the tellurometers and other instruments. An early form of snow mobile was used for transportation in the base camp area but they also did not take kindly to the cold temperatures.

Figure 24 Adam Kerr, US/Canada Weather Station at Isachsen, watercolour.

As with all surveys the first task was to determine the coordinates of the main geographical control. In this case it was planned to use an electronic transmitting system called Decca Lambda for positioning all the measurements of the data recorded. Using the system in such an inhospitable region was a ground breaking task. It required three transmitting stations to be built. Each station required heated accommodation for both the operational crew and the transmitting equipment. It also required antennas, 150 feet in height and a circular ground mat of wires of the same radius, associated with the antennas. I was personally involved in the surveys to provide the geographic positions of the transmitting stations. Several years previously a survey of points over all the islands of the archipelago had been carried out using a system called SHORAN. This provided a basic net work of positions but had to be linked to the Decca Lambda system and the task of the survey team was to link together the three transmitting stations with the SHORAN positions by means of a tellurometer traverse, as we had done earlier in Nova Scotia. I worked with Frank Hunt, a Newfoundland Land Surveyor who was remarkably tough. The routine was to measure the legs of a traverse across the frozen sea ice between each of the transmitting stations. The sea ice between the islands consists of a jumble of pressure ridges that were frozen solidly together and large pieces of ice were forced high in the air, Between the pressure ridges there were flat pieces of ice that were the result of the freezing of previous leads of open water in the ice. In the first year the surveyors flew between the stations on one of the fixed wing aircraft but as it was not always possible to land close to the stations the heavy equipment had to be carried for long distances over the snow. For this task we put on snow shoes to prevent us sinking into the soft snow between the ridges. Moreover the tellurometers did not function well in low temperatures and the survey ended up by having to set up the instruments in small heated tents, all of which had to be carried from the aircraft to the site. A potential problem that fortunately did not occur was an attack by polar bears. Initially the leader of the expedition was not convinced that the bears were a danger and advised the field parties that there was no need to carry rifles. Later it was found that these animals could be quite aggressive and members of the expedition had several close encounters. The overall work was to identify the highest pressure ridge and use these for points along the traverse, measuring distances between, typically about 5 miles, and the angle at each.

The work could be terribly cold with we surveyors having to keep a constant eye on our companion for the white blotch of frost bite on their cheeks. It was not a serious problem as by warming the spot with the back of your mitten it would quickly disappear but problems can occur when extremities are left untreated.

Landing with the small fixed wing aircraft on the frozen ice requires good judgement of the load bearing properties of the ice. During my time with the Project one of the Otter aircraft sank through the ice and the crew narrowly escaped with their lives by breaking through the ceiling of the aircraft and climbing out while it sank beneath the ice. Partly as a result of this problem and partly due to the logistic difficulties of getting closer to survey sites it was decided in the second year to employ helicopters. This greatly improved the team's abilities to carry out the survey traverses and to overcome many other logistical problems. Once the Decca Lambda stations had been put into operation navigation was mostly a matter of reading the coordinates off the receivers but prior to that more simple methods of navigation had to be adopted. The bush pilots of the light aircraft who had previously worked in tree covered more southern parts of Canada had carried out their navigation by becoming familiar with the area over which they flew. This might have included the whereabouts of a lake or even a certain tree. On coming to the open Arctic there were no trees and no lakes. Most of the area was a mass of white pressure ridges and frozen leads and it was difficult to distinguish one place from another. From my own experience as a marine navigator and also from reading a book by Keith Greenaway, an experienced navigator in the Royal Canadian Air Force (RCAF), I was able to show the pilots that in those very high latitudes the sun worked its way around the North Pole at a rate of 15 degrees of longitude per hour. Therefore by simply knowing the time, it was straightforward to calculate the sun's bearing. All the aircraft were fitted with gyro compasses which although not north seeking did maintain a fixed direction for at least an hour. Using the sun's direction by noting the time the compass could then be updated. So even though direction from a magnetic compass was not possible at least the pilots knew in which direction they were heading.

An important task using the Decca Lamba system of positioning was to calibrate it to measure the speed that the signals propagated across the frozen pack ice and the water on which it floated. Mike Eaton led this calibration, by observing the sun and astronomically working out the geographic position and comparing it with the Decca Lambda readings. One hazard of that operation was the risk of being blinded by the glare of the sun. This could be prevented by ensuring the correct shades were used on the telescope of the theodolite.

Having established a method of positioning both in support of navigation and as a reference for all the information collected, the work of gathering the data could begin. Fundamental to much of this, was knowledge of the depth of water and the hydrographic team was given some priority in that matter. A problem to be faced was how to measure depth beneath the ice which was at minimum 2 metres thick. Mike Eaton also took that task in hand with his first thought being that a hole could be blasted in the ice and a weighted line lowered to plumb the depth. Prior to going to the Arctic he had taken a course on handling explosives but in practice it was found that the method was not practical as the hole that was caused by the explosion was so shattered that it was difficult to get near unless some elaborate system of planks was used to bridge the broken up ice. Fortunately a scientist working at McGill University, Mike Marsden, discovered that acoustic energy could be sent through the ice and the sea beneath it to measure the depth. In practice the snow cover over the ice, which was normally only a few centimetres thick, could be removed and the echo sounder transducer placed firmly on the ice. Various questions had to be answered, such as the different propagation velocities of the acoustic signal through ice and water but ways could be found to overcome these problems. Initially Mike Eaton mounted his acoustic system on the back of a skidoo but later it was found that it could be deployed with a hydraulic probe used from a helicopter that could quickly land on the ice. During the 1980s, when I was in an administrative position in the Government, trials of unmanned vehicles that could be controlled to carry out the surveys under the ice without the need to penetrate the ice were carried out successfully. Our measurement of the depth over the continental shelf took place a few years after the first American submarines had made their epic transits under the ice to the North Pole and we were able to compare our own data with their bathymetric profiles under the ice.

Hydrography was not alone in carrying out field measurements. The physical properties of the water were measured by oceanographers. These were led by Art Collin, a physical oceanographer, who had joined the project and was later to become its leader. One of the earlier attempts to make observations using Nansan bottles for gathering sea samples was to find that as the metal bottles were taken from the relatively warm sea water in to the very cold air the metal bottles full of seawater froze and expanded so that they broke.

This necessitated future measurements being taken in the relative warmth of a heated tent. A rather more alarming part of the oceanographic programme was to have a polar bear charge the heated tent being used for oceanography. Fortunately on that camp a rifle was carried and was used to shoot this very large bear that dropped dead just a few metres from the tent. To this day Art Collin has the huge bear skin spread out on his living room floor. Geophysical measurements of gravity and magnetism were taken to help in a greater understanding of the underlying geology. This was also measured by the setting of explosive charges and using seismology.

In May the temperature became relatively mild and the snow on top of the ice began to melt and form puddles. These evaporated and caused low cloud to develop. This made flying very difficult and operations over the sea were much reduced. Although some of the scientists stayed on during the summer to carry out work that was mainly over the land it was time for most of the over ice hydrographic work to be terminated and for me to head south.

Another visit to the Sub-Arctic

After a brief visit to the office in Ottawa I was sent again to join the *Algerine* in Pictou and arrived there in mid June. While we were there some engineers from the National Research Council (NRC) fitted the ship with a new microwave positioning system that had been developed at the NRC. Once again the survey party headed to northern Newfoundland on 22 June where again it was to work in the area of Quirpon. On the way we went to the rescue of a broken down Icelandic trawler and towed it into Botwood on the west coast of Newfoundland. The survey in the area of Cape Bauld was a continuation of the previous year's work. This involved some further systematic sounding and the investigation of numerous shoal areas. This is a critical part of a hydrographic survey in which suspected shallow areas are carefully measured with an array of acoustic profiles' The operation is terminated by measuring the shallowest part by sounding with a weighted line to ensure the acoustic measurements have been correctly interpreted. Leaving that place on 23 July the ship called first at St Anthony, where there is a major Grenfell Mission hospital and I was able to meet Dr Thomas, the Director and some of the staff that my father had met when researching his Grenfell biography. Before I had come to Canada, my father had a contract from the International Grenfell Association to write a biography on the life of the medical missionary, Wilfred Grenfell.[9] He had originally worked with the Mission to Deep Sea Fishermen in the North Sea but had moved to Newfoundland and the Labrador to try to improve the welfare of the poor fishermen, who worked in many of the isolated out ports and were termed 'liveers'. He had established cooperatives, nursing stations and hospitals and at St Anthony was its main hospital and headquarters. My father, as a professional seaman, felt that Grenfell was rather rash, particularly in his boating activities but he clearly made a major contribution to the fortunes of the poor fishermen.

Some trouble with one of the ship's generators was experienced and it was decided that the ship must head south to Sydney on Cape Breton Island for repairs. *Algerine* arrived at Sydney at the end of July and while the repairs were undertaken we were free to amuse ourselves. Austin Quirk and I took one of the survey launches and went off to explore the Bras d'Or lakes, a beautiful area in the centre of Cape Breton Island. We entered the lakes through the Little Bras d'Or channel which is very narrow and scenic. In the middle of the area is the pretty little town of Badeck. This is

[9] J Lennox Kerr, *Wilfred Grenfell, his Life and Work*, 1959

famous as the home of Alexander Graham Bell, developer of the telephone. There is a museum dedicated to him and also a good yacht club where we surveyors were berated by one of the locals for not being able to speak the Gaelic, which is still spoken on the island, the heritage of the settlers from the Scottish Highlands. The Bras d'Or lakes are an almost totally enclosed fresh water area. Forests and gentle farm land surround the long lakes. The visit coincided with some very good weather and we were able to enjoy it as its best.

Once the repairs had been completed in mid August *Algerine* headed north keeping well to seaward of the Labrador coast, stopping along the way to carry out oceanographic measurements of temperature and salinity. We arrived off Resolution Island, which is on the southern extremity of Baffin Island and near the entrance to Frobisher Bay, which was the eventual destination. Unfortunately, as the ship was beginning to enter the long inlet there were further engine problems. In this case it was a broken piston. This could be repaired by the ship's engineers but as the ship was being carried towards a dangerous coast by the current the two survey launches were deployed to tow the ship out of danger. Eventually a Government icebreaker, the *Ernest Lapointe* came and towed *Algerine* to safety. Once the engine was repaired it was possible for us to make our own way but we had to deal with a lot of pack ice. By the end of August the ship had penetrated the ice belt and entered clear water and headed into Frobisher Bay, renamed Iqaluit in 1987. This was developing into a thriving settlement with an air strip. The domes of the US Radar Station overlook the town. Like many frontier towns Frobishers Bay was not attractive with much junk, in the form of empty oil drums and broken down snow mobiles littering the streets. There was a small commercial airport and various government buildings dominated the town. The native population was housed in small colourful wooden buildings. Smaller ships can get alongside the wharf at high tide but larger ships must lie at anchor and be discharged by barges. There are several good navigable channels through which ships can enter the port and our task was to survey these so that improved charts could be provided.

While most of the survey carried out the work by traditional means the new positioning system was being evaluated by the NRC engineers aboard. The angles that were traditionally measured by sextants were now measured electronically. While the system worked well enough it was overtaken by others that obtained distances measured electronically, such as Decca, Hi-Fix and LORAN. The presence of engineers from the NRC aboard led to many interesting discussions on other uses of technology that could improve the hydrographic surveyors' task. These included ideas for monitoring various parameters at different depths and improvements in the measurement of currents. As in Ungava Bay the tides were large, in the vicinity of 10 metres and the tidal currents were accordingly strong, although not as strong as those in Payne River. One day one of the launches ran aground on a pinnacle and at low tide was perched high in the air. When the tide went out huskies, which the Inuit kept on remote islands during the summer, decided to wade out from a nearby island to scrounge food scraps from the engineer who had stayed by the boat. As the tide rose again the dogs had to swim to get back to their island home.

After the basic surveys had been made the safest routes for shipping were identified and these were swept using the ship and its two survey launches and range marks erected. Interestingly some of these channels have been given very American names from patrons of earlier expeditions, such as the Cinnicinati Press Channel. The main shipping channel was called the Pike-Resor Channel. While the islands near the shipping channels are comparatively low there is a range of very high mountains on the south side

Frobisher Bay is historically important because it was here that Martin Frobisher thought he had discovered gold in 1576. He returned on a second voyage and carried home a large quantity of ore only to find that it was in fact only iron pyrites or fool's gold. On board during this second year on *Algerine* there were some changes in the survey crew. Dick LeLievre, an Acadian French Canadian, remained as the survey chief and with experience had become a little more relaxed. A young French Canadian had also joined the party. He was ill equipped for the rough life of a survey ship with a background as a librarian. He had married a pretty girl just before leaving on the trip. She clearly held the purse strings as their private conversations were carried over the ship and launch radios and we could all hear their discussions and disputes about their problems of borrowing money. Poor Andre, after we returned to civilisation their marriage broke up and he returned to a more suitable occupation. As had been the practice the previous year the charterers provided rum on Saturday nights and we continued to enjoy the excellent curries made by Austin Quirk from the locally acquired game in the form of geese and hares. A memory of that time was rowing ashore in one of the dories, on a cold autumn morning, to try to shoot the birds. The mate, a rotund little man, who seemed to ooze fat out of every pore, accompanied some of us in the dory to try to shoot some geese. While we complained bitterly of the cold his layer of fat seemed to completely insulate him from it! The hunting party got ashore and climbed the hill behind which the honking of geese could be heard. When we could see the row of geese heads we ducked down and at a signal our group all rose up and fired our rifles. Surely some must have been hit? But as we watched the whole flock went gliding away over the tundra. Sadly, there was nothing for the pot that night!

On 8 October, with the weather deteriorating rapidly it was time to leave Frobisher Bay and head south for Nova Scotia. This time the ship went to Halifax, where the organisation was beginning to move its field headquarters from Pictou. By good fortune my old friend Harry Wolfe, whose wife had been a passenger on a Blue Funnel ship many years ago, was in Halifax as an engineering officer on a British submarine. Needless to say it was a cause to celebrate, although going into the bowels of a submarine, even though it was on the surface, to drink horses' necks – a mixture of brandy and ginger ale - was a hard way to cure a hangover!

In mid October I returned to Ottawa but was almost immediately sent out again to participate in a survey of Kingston Harbour. This is a fine little town on the shore of Lake Ontario where later I was to spend much time. Amongst other institutions it is the home of the Canadian Royal Military College and also Queen's University and the large Kingston Penitentiary. The weather remained fine enough to be able to survey the sheltered harbour but by the end of November it was time to close down field operations for the winter months. There was some incentive for putting in a lengthy part of the year in the field. Not only was I a bachelor enjoying free accommodation while in the field but there was a system of bonuses for field work – a huge $ 300 – and it was possible to get a double bonus for an extended field season.

As I had then been in Canada for nearly two years I felt it was time to go back to England for Christmas and to see my family. I flew back on the same plane as my friend Mike Eaton and remember his comment as we circled before landing at Prestwick in Scotland. 'For the last two years we have criticised everything in Canada and compared them with the good things in the United Kingdom and now we shall land in England and compare everything with the good things in Canada'. How true that was but in retrospect I found the general attitude in Canada, particularly in the work, was the 'can do' attitude. This was particularly important as a young man. I had realised from the start of my work in Canada that you could have experience by the boatload but unless you had a university degree you would not progress far, at least working for the Federal Government. I therefore started looking into ways to get into university. Here I came up against a brick wall. I went to see the Registrar at Carleton University in Ottawa. He essentially told me that to get a place in the university I had to have formal entry qualifications, which in Canada was senior matriculation. My extra Conway certificate, supposed to be equivalent to senior matriculation in the United Kingdom and my Foreign Going Master Mariner's certificate, which qualified me to be Captain of the largest merchant ship, were not accepted in lieu of the formal qualification. That has now changed with numerous ways to get mature entrance into university but at that time in Canada the only course open to me was to pass the senior matriculation exams. To this I gave my attention in whatever free time was available. In my diary I note that I spent three or four hours each weekday evening on these studies.

As well as being a student in the evenings I was also a teacher during the days. In addition to the task of processing the field data from the summer survey I was assigned to help a new training section that had been set up. Prior to the introduction of recruiting mariners most of the surveyors had a background in civil engineering and were capable in land surveying. To equip new mariners and recruits from other backgrounds with the knowledge needed to carry out the hydrographic surveys the organisation established an in house training section. This was led by Sid Van Dyck but I had some responsibility marking papers and giving lectures on subjects, such as astronomy, that were familiar to me from my sea going days.

It is not possible to go into detail all my activities during the winter months. I became an avid skier at the nearby station of Camp Fortune in the Gatineau Hills in Quebec. I enjoyed a great friendship with Mike Eaton and we skied together often. I had a girl friend, Barbara Blount, who joined us in the skiing and social life but it does not seem to have been a lasting affair. Occasionally we would go on the winding and rough road to Mont Tremblant where there was excellent skiing and very good French Canadian cuisine. I also got to know Fred Roots, the leader of the Polar Shelf Project, and his wife June and their family on a social level. Through this relationship I was also in contact with several of the scientists involved with the PCSP project and other polar activities. This included Geoffery Hattersly-Smith and his Greek wife Maria. He had previously been with the FIDS organisation.

Later in the winter we were busy getting ready for the Polar Shelf field programme once again. Drills and other equipment had to be tested. On 14 March 1960 I was off again to the far North. My daily log begins to record temperatures of – 35 degrees Fahrenheit. The weather that year was particularly unkind and there were considerable difficulties in getting supplies transhipped through Resolute. The project was using a Bristol freight aircraft and at times an Avro York in addition to the smaller DeHaviland Otters. The Herman Nelson heaters, which blasted hot air into the engine to warm them up to get them started were in full use.

I spent much of this period in Resolute helping to expedite the stores moving through to Isachsen. We employed some of the local Inuit for a time with the loading of the aircraft but they were unreliable because when the hunting was good they disappeared.

With the weather showing signs of improving some field work was started but it was extremely cold. Frequent blizzards moved through the area making outside work difficult. Repairs to the aircraft had to be carried out under wretched conditions and at times we had to employ local Inuit to build snow walls to offer some protection. If the weather was fine in Resolute it was bad in Isachsen and vice versa. I did not get away from Resolute and up to Isachsen until 20 April. The Decca Lambda stations were being put into operation with the crews installed in Parcoll Huts, a type of insulated Nissan Hut that were well heated and generally comfortable with a floor area of 20 by 16 feet. Some particular problems associated with installing the transmitting stations included the need to secure the 150 feet tall masts on the permafrost. To penetrate the frozen ground in order to insert the large bolts that were needed to secure the guy wires required either a special drill or a flame thrower. The job was eventually done and the field parties could now obtain precise locations for their data and for their navigation over the entire area of the continental shelf off the Canadian Arctic Archipelago. Accommodation for some of the field parties was a lot less comfortable than at the main base station in Isachsen or at the Decca sites. In the field stations accommodation was mainly in Mount Logan tents, double walled tents that could be kept reasonably warm with the use of the small Coleman fuel stoves. Never the less on waking up in the morning your head and beard poking out through your sleeping bag had a rime of ice. I was once again working on the Tellurometer traverse across the sea ice to connect the three Decca stations together with my tough Newfoundland colleague, Frank Hunt, who seemed quite impervious to the cold. Life was made a bit easier in the second year by the use of helicopters, which could deposit the surveyors and their equipment close to the large pressure ridges on which we took our measurements. Different kinds of scientific data were being gathered with oceanographic teams out on the ice and various geophysical measurements being taken. The good weather window was short lived and towards the end of May it again deteriorated with blizzards and low cloud arriving as the temperatures warmed and the sea ice melted on top and became puddled. This all resulted in much low stratus cloud making flying conditions extremely difficult. On 29 May I was on my way south again, this time through Uranium City and Edmonton.

This year I travelled south through Edmonton and I was able to spend some time in that part of Canada, where I had relatives, before taking a few days in Ottawa then heading off once more to join a chartered sealing vessel in Halifax. This was a change of ship, the *Theron*, A Norwegian flagged ship that had previously made an epic voyage to the Antarctic under its experienced Captain Harald Maro.

Figure 25 Charter Ship *Theron.*

For the third year the survey headed again for northern Newfoundland where the working area was to the west of Cape Bauld in the vicinity of Cape Onion. The two survey launches and the survey crew remained basically unchanged. The same routine of establishing the geodetic control on shore and then the launch and ship were used to carry out the hydrographic surveys along the coast. My notes of this time seem to dwell as much on the excellent fishing for brook trout and sea trout that could be found in the nearby streams and estuaries as of the survey activities. During the days we had to cope with the numerous mosquitoes and black flies on land and the rough seas in the launches but in the evenings and weekends we could get away to go fishing.

My journal does not record a most interesting meeting we had while at Cape Onion. A Norwegian couple arrived on board that later turned out to be the Norwegian explorer Helge Ingstad and his daughter, to ask the Norwegian Captain if they could borrow the ship's lifeboat to explore a site nearby that they thought was an early Viking settlement. This turned out to be the settlement at L'Anse aux Meadows that became a World Heritage site in 1978, where they found the remains of several long houses and other artefacts that established this as the first known settlement of the Vikings in North America, dating back approximately 1000 years. We surveyors had fished close to the area as it was near a good trout stream, but our untrained eyes had failed to detect any man made remains. It was Helge Ingstad's wife Anne Stine, who was the archaeologist who had done the research necessary to locate the site. Following the annual routine, by late July, the ice was considered to have sufficiently cleared to start progress north. We rounded Cape Chidley on 23 July and entered Hudson Straits.

This year, 1960, the party surveyed along the south coasts of Hudson Strait. One of the Hydrographic Services' large survey ships *Baffin* was surveying the central part of the main channel that leads into Hudson Bay. The task of the *Theron* was to chart some of the harbours and inshore waters along the southern coast of the strait. When the ship arrived there was still some sea ice barring the way but the ship worked through this and arrived at Wakeham Bay, a fine harbour surrounded by steep bare hills reaching up

1,500 feet above sea level. There was a small Hudson's Bay store and about 30 Inuit tents nearby. Following the usual routine the party had to establish the control ashore. A tide gauge was installed so that all the depth measurements could be reduced to a common level. Geographic control was brought down into the bay from a series of high points that had been established by land surveyors, using SHORAN, some years before. This was hard work as survey markers and instruments had to be carried on our shoulders from the shoreline up to the marks over a thousand feet above. Every morning a survey launch would drop us at the foot of a hill and we would spend the day climbing up to the mark, and measuring the angles with theodolites, before returning to the shore later in the day. It was hot climbing up and usually very windy taking the observations at the survey mark. Fortunately there were no black flies and fewer mosquitoes than there had been in Newfoundland. On one occasion Andre Menier, our young French Canadian surveyor, was not there when the launch went to pick him up in the late afternoon. The launch waited for several hours but eventually decided to go back to the ship for dinner and get on with processing the work. Meanwhile the launch was sent back to wait for Andre. At about ten o'clock, the launch arrived back with a bedraggled and sad looking Andre. He was sent off for his dinner and the other surveyors took his survey notes to develop the mean angles. Theodolites at that time were very difficult to level and easily disturbed. Changes of temperature and any other disturbance could affect the level and thus the precision of the measurements.

In the remarks of Andre's survey notes was the comment; 'Kicked the instrument by mistake and then kicked it again on purpose.' He had clearly had a difficult day on the mountain.

Fishing for the abundant Arctic char was a major pre-occupation of the surveyors and crew in Wakeham Bay and in fact much of the Sub-Arctic. While the surveyors were mainly interested in fishing as a recreational pursuit the Norwegian crew tackled the matter more professionally with nets. *Theron* had a hold that could be refrigerated so the many fish caught could be frozen down to keep until the ship returned South again. The Arctic char is, like the salmon, a fine fighting fish and gave us all much enjoyment to catch. Although I tried fly fishing in the rivers and lakes the use of lures in the estuaries proved to be the most rewarding.

The survey party moved westwards to Douglas Harbour, another inlet on this fjord like coast, which was also surrounded by high hills. The stop there was short before pushing on to Sugluk, a little further west. It was quite a large settlement and there with a large number of Inuit tents, a well kept Hudson's Bay post and a Roman Catholic Church and Mission. The encouragement of the local people to carve soap stone figures and ornaments had spread from Cape Dorset on Baffin Island to other Arctic settlements. At that time the Inuit were happy to exchange their carvings for old clothes but once the demand had been established the carvings became expensive to buy. My friend Mike Eaton, when surveying in the Belcher Islands had discovered the availability of these carvings which were carved from attractive green stone. In Sugluk the natives made carvings out of both green soapstone and much whiter limestone. I have a small collection of carvings collected at Sugluk, Deception Bay and other settlements. Soapstone is fairly soft and easy to carve and subsequently I found that the material is used by carvers in many other parts of the World, including Africa. Finally moving westward along the south coast of Hudson Strait, the ship stopped at Deception Bay. The Hudson Bay post was abandoned, an old graveyard told of white mans' passing and some remains from a mining company were to be seen. The stay in Sugluk and Deception Bay was marred by frequent storms and by mid September snow was beginning to move down the mountains towards sea level. By the end of the month field work was becoming increasingly difficult and much time was spent aboard processing data. In spite of the weather occasions were found to go fishing, both in the sea and by walking across the tundra to inland lakes and streams. On 30 September the ship headed home and rounded Cape Chidley, the most northern point of Labrador, and headed south. We passed Saglek and the magnificent Torngat Mountains could be seen to the west. We stopped at Hopedale midway down the Labrador coast to await further instructions. While there some local surveys were carried out, working with the *Arctic Sealer*, another chartered vessel. At Hopedale there were the remains of a large Moravian Missionary station and a small settlement. Eventually orders were received and the survey were instructed to head for Halifax, where *Theron* arrived on 11 October.

I returned to Ottawa with Austin Quirk by car. It was a pleasant drive. The fall colours were mainly over but our trip took us through the attractive northern USA states of Maine, New Hampshire and Vermont. My field work was not over and I was sent to join the survey ship *Kapuskasing* in the Gulf of St Lawrence to position the masts for a new Decca chain that was being established. I joined the ship in Sept Iles on the north coast of the St Lawrence Estuary. On my way there I had stopped in Montreal to spend a little time with Angela Woodfield, my old friend Tom Woodfield's sister. During that period, survey work was carried out in several remote parts of the Gulf. Anticosti Island, 217 miles in length, in the middle of the Gulf, besides being totally owned by a large paper company, was a haven for many wild deer, which had been introduced into the island in the 1920s. The ship also went to Natasquan, a small settlement with a large Indian population on the north side of the Gulf. With the survey over the ship went to Sydney, Nova Scotia and it was time for me to return for another winter in Ottawa.

This time in Ottawa was memorable for me for two matters, my affair with Shirley Bond and my determination to complete my studies and acquire the senior matriculation necessary to get into university. Shirley Bond or the 'glorious red head', as I refer to her in my journal, was the cause of a serious infatuation during that winter. I intended to marry her which caused concern for my parents in distant England. It went as far as a proposal but the romance fell apart in the spring. I had met Shirley through my friend Art Collin and he also introduced me to Vic Sims, a geographer, living in

Ottawa. A great memory of these two friends was skiing with them at Mount Washington in New Hampshire. We celebrated the end of the skiing season first at Stowe in Vermont, where a group of us used to ski and carouse and then for the long May weekend, when all the snow had gone locally in Canada we would go to Mount Washington. When I first went there we would camp halfway up the mountain and then go on to ski in a glacial cirque further up the mountain. Later the authorities forbade camping in Tuckerman's Ravine at the base of the glacial cirque due to too much drug and alcohol use by the skiers. At that time of the year the days are quite warm and it froze at night. The result was to produce wonderful sugar snow. There were no ski tows and we had to climb up with our skis on our shoulders. The braver you were the higher up the head wall at the top of the cirque you climbed. The ultimate was to ski down the very steep gullies above the head wall. On one occasion our little party set off too early in the morning and the sugar snow was still frozen and we lost our footing and slid a long way down the steep slope on our backs. The weekend was dominated by the antics of 'crazy' French Canadians as this was a Canadian holiday and many skiers went there from Quebec Province. Another person I met during that winter was an American Barbara Rost, who worked at the US Embassy and through her I met the three rather lovely daughters of the Venezuelan Ambassador. We all went on a trip to New York, which was an eye opening experience – my first trip to that great city. Barbara, whose family lived in that city was an excellent guide and took us to see both some of its fine art galleries and its rougher night spots.

My determination to get into university drove me to acquire the necessary Senior Matriculation. I sat for the Cambridge entrance exams but I was clearly not ready for the academic life and failed. At that time the Canadian Department of Veterans Affairs was still supporting the military personnel returning from the war, in particular from the Korean war, to help get them into university. It had established a system of correspondence courses and it was these that I chose to follow. The actual exams for Senior Matriculation were scheduled for the end of the school year in June and this meant that rather than go up to the high Arctic in March, as in previous years, I was given assignments in the Ottawa area to study and eventually sit the exams, which I successfully passed. My supervisors were supportive of the plan and arranged for me to work on local surveys of the Ottawa River. So in 1961 I did not head up to the Arctic until the end of June.

A Third Year in the Arctic, 1961

The work this year was quite different from my previous northern adventures. I travelled up to the Arctic via Calgary, where I visited a Cornish cousin and her husband. This provided a chance to see something of the Rocky Mountains. I visited Banff and swam in the sulphur pools. From Calgary I moved on to Yellowknife – very much a frontier town in those days. On 2 July I boarded a Bristol freighter that the expedition had chartered and headed for Cambridge Bay on the south side of the Arctic Archipelago. We had some excitement leaving Cambridge Bay because in addition to me flying as a passenger in the navigator's seat we were loaded down with a cargo of explosives to be used in the seismic activities. As we were taxiing down the runway the pilot decided that one of the engines was faulty and the brakes had to be slammed on. I watched as the end of the run way get closer and closer. Fortunately we came to a halt before we reached it and the main damage was to the brake linings of the under carriage. The engine problem proved to be minor. Across the Archipelago to Resolute summer had set in and there was little snow on the land areas and the sea ice was much broken up. The open ocean was puddled and consequently causing much low cloud and difficult flying conditions over the ice covered sea areas.

Eventually I arrived at Resolute and once more arrived in Isachsen, where I linked up with my fellow surveyors Mike Eaton and Neil Anderson. The weather at that time of year although considerably warmer than it had been in the spring of previous years, was unstable with frequent storms passing through. The hydrographic work depended mainly on helicopters. These were chartered and ranged from the small Bell Jet Rangers to the much larger Sikorsky 55. The surveys were initially of local areas around Ellef Ringnes Island. Radio communications with the main base at Isachsen and the fly camps was very erratic. Problems with the ionosphere caused the radio difficulties. Isachsen itself was a sea of mud. Landing the fixed wing aircraft in places away from the main camp was difficult due to the soft ground. During that time through ice surveys were made of promising future sites for ports, such as Malloch Dome, although it was to be quite a number of years before ships, even icebreakers could reach these places.

Towards the end of July the survey operation was moved to the critical Belcher Channel that leads north of Devon Island, through Norwegian Bay and eventually to the western fjords of Ellesmere Island. This was an area that icebreakers were able to penetrate during the most ice free part of the year to reach Eureka. Historically the straits are named after Captain Edward Belcher, who led one of the main search parties looking for the ill fated Captain Franklin. Indeed while the survey team was in camp besides the straits we found a number of interesting artefacts from his camps of the mid nineteenth century. These included broken pieces of clay pipe and some rusty tin cans with a brass label soldered on the outside that bore the caption 'Boiled Beef, Cheapside 1840.' The survey went slowly due to the frequent storms and although it was then high summer my log records mention of frequent snow storms and high winds.

Accommodation during the survey was in Mount Logan tents. Provided they are heated by Coleman stoves they are warm and comfortable. However to quote from the log " A most miserable night, woke up to find myself lying in a pool of water. The edge of my cot had been touching the edge of the tent. It blew and poured with rain overnight. This morning there was thick fog that persisted on and off all day with occasional short clearings. We have all spent the day reading, writing and being generally lazy.'

On the last day of July a message was received from the main base saying that the Minister urgently required a survey of the south coast of Melville Island. The instructions were to finish the Belcher Channel as quickly as possible and return to Isachsen to restructure equipment. The new survey was to be carried out between Bridport Inlet and Winter Harbour. This was approximately 400 miles south west of Isachsen. Historically this area was important because it was at Winter Harbour that Captain Edward Parry spent two years in 1820-22 with the ships *Erebus* and *Terror*. Captain Parry had made a remarkable penetration of the North West Passage through the major channel that now bears his name. Unfortunately he was unable to extricate his ships from the ice after his first winter and had to spend an additional and unplanned winter in the area. At the beginning of August we moved to Bridport Inlet and established camp. The main objective of the survey was to precisely position the coordinates for a prospective oil drilling operation. While it had been predicted by geologists several years before on Operation Franklin that there was a good possibility of finding hydrocarbons in the Arctic Archipelago, this was to be the first attempt to carry out exploratory drilling. The establishment of the position for the drilling site by the survey team was to be by conventional land surveying with theodolites and Tellurometers used to extend the geographic control from established points.

In the area of our camp at Winter Harbour there are several important historical sites. Bridport Inlet is the site of an historical post office on Dealey Island. There is a large cairn, suitably marked with a post and barrel in which passing ships left messages. These included messages from Sergeant Henry Larsen, who had taken the Royal Canadian Mounted Police ship *St Roch* through the North West Passage in 1940-42. In another cairn, some three miles inland, at Table Hill we found further information and messages from Captain Bernier. He was a French Canadian who had great plans to reach the North Pole in 1908. Amongst the papers was a page torn out of Hansard recording his speech to the Canadian Parliament in which he declared that he would be the first to reach the North Pole At Winter Harbour there is a stone building that still contains the rotten bags of coal that had been stored there. On the beach there were memorials to three of the crew of HMS *Resolute* ,marked by three elaborately carved wooden tombstones made from ship's hatch boards. The three unfortunate sailors whose deaths were recorded on these monuments had all been very young and it is tragic to think of them dying in this remote place. The whole area has been visited by many of the early explorers and they have left numerous cairns and monuments to record their presence. It is the choke point of numerous attempts to get through the North West Passage. To the west was McClure Strait, which until recently has been blocked by ice that was impossible to penetrate by the sailing vessels of the day. To the southwest was the much narrower Prince of Wales Strait, which eventually was found to provide a route linking the Parry Channel with the Beaufort Sea to the west.

The survey work proceeded well except our American helicopter pilot was convinced that wolves presented a hazard to the crew. This was disregarded until walking along a dry stream bed we came across the tracks of a pack of large wolves. Fortunately, we did not encounter them. The work was completed within a week and the party was once again off to Isachsen on 12 August and then on to complete some of the local hydrographic surveys around Ellef Ringnes Island. Looking back on my log books of that time they recorded not only the frequent bad weather but also the incredibly erratic hours we worked to take advantage of good weather when it occurred. Starting a day's work at two or three in the morning was quite commonplace. The fact that there was 24 hours of daylight meant that we were not controlled by the clock.

Later in August, the tie was made between the real world of ship navigation, and surveying remote areas of solid sea ice that would be unlikely to see a ship for many years. I flew to Eureka on Ellesmere Island, which at that time was the most northern base station and was being visited by the powerful icebreaker *John A Macdonald.* This ship was less than a year old and represented the Canadian Government's policy development towards the Arctic. It was 6180 tons and had powerful 18,000 horse power engines. The Captain was called Cuthbert, a Scot. One of the hydrographers, Harvey Blandford, had been one of the founding members of the

Polar Shelf Project, was already aboard. It was my task to help record the soundings as the ship entered virtually unexplored territory. The area of Ellesmere Island and Axel Heiberg Island to the west, are much more mountainous than the terrain around Ellef Ringnes. The fjord like coastline is most scenic, with steep cliffs on each side and apparently good deep water in the channel. A matter to be considered is that visible high mountains above the sea may also be reflected in undetected high peaks beneath the adjacent sea and a ship moving through such poorly surveyed waters needs to be extremely cautious in its navigation. The ship steadily moved southwards passing through such critical passages as Norwegian Bay and Hell's Gate. During this meandering journey, much new information was collected. Apart from data collected by the ship itself we made sorties in the ship's helicopter and the hydrographic launch to explore various potential small harbours and straits. We arrived at Resolute on September 1 where I was put ashore. After several days I was flown out to the survey ship *Baffin* to begin another phase of the saga.

Baffin was a powerful survey ship that carried six survey launches and two helicopters. It was the most capable ship in the World for working in ice covered waters. Its function in 1961 was to systematically survey Lancaster Sound which led into Barrow Strait. This is the main entrance of the Parry Channel that leads into the North West Passage. One of our tasks was to geographically link the islands on each side of this wide strait. Distances of over fifty miles were measured in a system of trilateration across the straits. This tested our surveying capabilities to the full as well as making full use of the two small helicopters that we carried on board.

Figure 26 CSS *Baffin* in Lancaster Sound.

The ship carried over twenty surveyors who were involved in a large range of work. The surveyor in charge was D'Arcy Charles, who had considerable Arctic experience.

Like so many parts of the Arctic that I visited Lancaster Sound was steeped in history. Foremost of this was Beechey Island on the south west corner of the coast of Devon Island, where Franklin had wintered in his first year before disappearing The remains of his crew were found many years later on King William Island, some distance to the south. So much has been discovered since I visited the area in 1961. Then the story of the unfortunate Captain Franklin and his ill fated crew was not well known. Over the years since my visit graves of some of his crew have been dug up on Beechey Island and remains of his crew trying to escape to the northern mainland of Canada have been found on King William Island. Recently, in 2014 the wreck of one of his ships that was crushed by the pack ice has been located. Lancaster Sound was also an important working area of the many whalers during the eighteenth and nineteenth century. At Port Leopold on the south side of the Straits, which we visited by helicopter during our survey operations there was much evidence of the once active whaling industry. The old Hudson's Bay building was still intact and the shoreline was littered with old whale bones, the iron hoops left over from the barrels that had been used to store the oil and bits of coal left from heating the try pots still remained. Although not much in evidence during *Baffin's* visit there were the remains of camp sites that showed that the local Inuits often visited Port Leopold. Although the larger whales were not in evidence at that time there were numerous sightings of narwhal and belugas.

In mid September the ice was showing signs of freezing and it was time for the ship to move south. We passed through Baffin Bay, an historic whaling ground, keeping a good way off the coast of Baffin Island. The weather, although getting cooler was generally kind and I note ' Very scenic this morning with the distant snow covered mountains showing wonderfully pink in the sun.' Besides working up the data from our surveys I spent some leisure time doing a large water colour sketch of the ship as a commission for Barry McDonald, the assistant chief surveyor. Later the sketch was used to reproduce Christmas cards.

At the end of September *Baffin* reached the Lady Franklin Islands, a desolate group of high steep rocks off the south east coast of Baffin Island. The task was to obtain a precise position for the islands and their relationship to the nearby coast Fortunately the helicopters saved the surveyors from the task of scaling these peaks. A potential hazard of the operation was the presence of polar bears but fortunately they found it as difficult to scale the peaks as did we surveyors. On one occasion I was measuring some angles on the top of the islands when a large mother bear and three cubs landed at the foot.

Figure 27 Adam Kerr with Wild T3 Theodolite.

Fortunately they made no attempt to climb the steep face. While surveying another group of these isolated islands, the Monumental Group, there was a tremendous herd of walrus as well as more polar bears. During all this work and during my entire time on *Baffin*, I worked with a surveyor, Ross Douglas, who later became the Dominion Hydrographer, a close associate and friend. Surveys to position these offshore groups of islands and rocks continued until 9 October when the snow was beginning to hinder the survey and the land looking bleak and white. Civilisation was beckoning and I noted that I shaved off my beard. It actually was not much of a beard and it was later in my life that I could grow a full set. The ship worked slowly south along the coast of Labrador doing small surveys and checking anomalies in the charts. We visited Saglek, Battle Harbour and other small outposts on this rugged coast. On 19 October the ship finally arrived in Halifax and the survey was disbanded. I flew to Ottawa and during a brief visit met Liv Esbensen, a Norwegian girl working at their Embassy, who was later to become my first wife. By the end of the month I returned to *Baffin* as the third mate. This was partly to fill a vacancy and partly to keep my hand in as a navigator. This was a relatively short oceanographic cruise working in the Gulf Stream, 350 miles off the coast of Nova Scotia. In mid November I was back in Ottawa having completed a very full season in the field.

Winter of 1961-62

My pattern of life showed a significant change from previous years. While in the Arctic I had received an invitation to share a house with a Norwegian called Ragnar Narum. This invitation had been engineered by Peter Wadell, who worked for the same large paper company as Ragnar. The house was located in the Gatineau Hills in the Province of Quebec and just north of Ottawa. It is a beautiful area and the house was close to the Gatineau River, a tributary of the larger Ottawa River. It was also close to the network of ski slopes and trails that made it attractive to Ragnar, who as a Norwegian was an enthusiastic skier. Over the years while he had lived and worked in the Ottawa area Ragnar had collected a large group of friends. These were mainly Scandinavians but also included many other European expatriates. He claimed to have been brutally treated by the Nazis during the war years and was at least twenty years older than I was. He was certainly the life and soul of the party and loved to drink and carouse. Over the years he had shared the house with other bachelors but each one had eventually got married. It was my turn next. The house in Kirk's Ferry was owned by people that went to Florida every winter and were happy to have someone to look after it. It was an ideal arrangement for us as it was an easy commute into our offices in Ottawa and a good place to spend the weekends. Ragnar had whittled down some old wooden skis into the narrow skis used for touring or cross country skiing. He would take me out to help him cross check the racing trails. This was before skidoos became popular and available and it was necessary to break down the heavy snow on the trails before races could take place. In the evenings Ragnar and I would gather in the little house to eat, drink and make merry. The agreement was that Ragnar would cook the fish and I would cook the meat. All this was, of course, washed down with large quantities of alcohol. Aquavit was a favoured tipple and this was drunk with much formal skaaling. In early March there were the ski jumping championships at Camp Fortune. One of the group, Colin Bergh, whose father was Norwegian, was a ski jumper and we would be at the ski jump to cheer him on. Also in the spring there was an annual pilgrimage to Stowe in Vermont over the Easter to enjoy the Spring skiing and the sugar snow.

I was in close contact with Art Collin and was beginning to build my relationship with Liv Esbensen, who was from the extreme north of Norway at Vadso. Together we skied regularly at local resorts, including Mont Tremblant in Quebec. Encouraged by Peter Waddell, before the skiing season started I was involved in playing some rugby although our team, the Bytown Beavers could not have been very good as I note that in November I had driven to Montreal and played a game at which we lost 25-0!

For Christmas that year I flew back to the UK again to spend time with my parents and various friends in Cornwall. On New Year's Eve my parents had been invited to a party given by a local artist, John Tunnard and it snowed to a depth of 4 inches, something almost unheard of in that part of the country and needless to say stopped everyone from getting to the party. I also found time to go up to North Wales before I returned to Canada, to give a talk to the cadets at my old training ship of *Conway.*

Figure 28 Log cabin beside the Gatineau River.

By mid January I was back in Ottawa . It was during that period that Liv and I and our good friends the Berghs decided that we would buy 60 acres of land on the east side of the Gatineau River. The land was a mixture of rocky land covered in maple trees and land cultivated to grow hay. Initially we thought we should manage the hay crop ourselves but we soon found that we lacked the knowledge to be farmers and harvested the hay as a standing crop under a contract with the adjacent farmer. We later bought a small traditional log farm building that we took apart and reconstructed on our land. In the nineteenth century many similar cabins had been made from the white pine which covered that part of the country. We carefully numbered the logs, which had been squared by axe and were joined at the corners by a tongue and groove construction. We replaced the roof with wooden cedar shingles. Heated by a wood burning stove it made an excellent residence that we used summer and winter, swimming in the river in the summer and skiing across it during the winter. The Berghs had intended to build a similar cabin but were slow to start it and in the end we bought their logs from them and used them to build a traditional sauna with an old wood stove to heat it and a grass roof on top in true Scandinavian style. We had great enjoyment in our cabin. The white doorway I painted with a Norwegian floral design called Rosemaling. In the spring we tapped the maple trees to collect maple sap, which we heated to make rather smoky syrup. Ragnar and I had decided to construct GP 14 sailing dinghies in the basement of a house that Liv and I were renting. Ragnar was a much more painstaking shipwright than I was but I quickly led the way to launch our boat on the Gatineau River.

The winter was not all play and no work. Some of my colleagues and I had persuaded our superiors that the roles of navigating officers should be combined with that of the hydrographic surveyors. This was the way it was structured in most other countries, including the United Kingdom. Canada had developed on different lines with the hydrographic surveyors being recruited with civil engineering backgrounds and having no direct experience as navigators and the ships 'being driven' by certificated navigators with no hydrographic training. We argued that this split form of command was not cost effective and in fact had probably been responsible for the *Baffin* on its maiden voyage to be run aground on an isolated rock off Nova Scotia, due to a difference of opinion between the navigating and hydrographic teams. Our managers were persuaded that the system of combining the roles should be tried out and I, with my master mariner's certificate and my increasing knowledge of hydrography, was appointed to command a small survey ship *Cartier*. On the Pacific coast another hydrographer with similar qualifications, Tom McCulloch, was appointed to command *Richardson that* was to be employed on surveys in the Western Arctic. To me this was all quite thrilling as I was only in my late twenties and my father was exceedingly proud of his sailor son. *Cartier* was based in Nova Scotia but I remained in Ottawa during the winter to continue as a training assistant and also to oversee the various administrative matters associated with my new command.

During the winter Ragnar re-introduced me to Liv Esbensen. As a true Norwegian Liv loved skiing and all her country's traditions and so it was just a matter of time for the relationship to thicken and for us to spend an increasing time together at Kirk's Ferry. However the developing relationship had to cope with the fact that the responsibilities of the *Cartier in*volved long distances and periods apart, although in the early summer I brought the

Cartier up the St Lawrence River and into the Great Lakes and I was then rather closer to Ottawa and Liv.

SURVEY SHIP *CARTIER*

I was in command of *Cartier* but the ship was to be used as a training ship and Mike Bolton, a more senior surveyor, was in overall charge of the training. The programme was to spend half the summer in the more docile conditions of the Great Lakes, based at Kingston on Lake Ontario and half the summer on the tidal and generally more complex St Lawrence River. It was a great experience for me. Although the ship was quite small, with a length of 140 feet, being converted from a wooden motor minesweeper built at Midland, Ontario during the War, it carried two survey launches and a crew, including over twenty trainees.

Figure 29 CSS *Cartier* in the Thousand Islands.

Travelling up and down the St Lawrence Seaway the ship passed through the huge locks and was completely dwarfed by the large lakers, carrying iron ore and grain and over 700 feet in length. In the St Lawrence River the programme was carried out below Quebec City in the area of Riviere du Loup. This is a turbulent part of the river with a large tidal range and very strong currents. It also had occasional heavy fog as a result of the mixing of the waters of different temperatures, particularly where the Saguenay River, a deep fjord like tributary entered the St Lawrence River. After the first year in command of *Cartier* I took the ship to Kingston where it was to spend the winter undergoing its annual refit. I was appointed to work for the Ships' Division under Rear Admiral Storrs. This was a different experience and apart from regular inspection trips to Kingston to supervise the work going on with *Cartier* I worked on a career strategy that was designed to develop combined hydrographers and navigating officers. To my regret the plan of combining the ship's officers with the hydrographic surveyors was never put in place and the idea of a combined role for the Canadian hydrographic surveyors never came to fruition. The problem was that most of the recruits came from engineering or surveying backgrounds and these did not have marine qualifications. The latter took several years to acquire the sea time and this did not fit in well with the career progressions as planned in the Hydrographic Service. For a short time the system was reintroduced when a Newfoundlander, Julian Goodyear, with a good engineering degree and marine qualifications was given a command of the *Mathew* working around Newfoundland.

The winter of 1962- 63 saw the relationship between Liv and I develop and Liv moved into the house in the Gatineau which Ragnar and I shared. In March 1963 we married in Horten, Norway. Unfortunately a short while before the wedding I received word from my mother that my father was seriously ill and they could not attend. It was decided that our marriage should still go ahead and I went to spend some time with my parents. My father was in hospital. The wedding was in the Garrison Church in Horten, not far from Oslo . Sadly the groom's side of the church was empty. The wedding ceremony was carried out in true Norwegian style with a magnificent banquet with white table cloths and glittering silver and shining glasses. Appropriate 'skaals' were raised. The following day, with cross country skis on our shoulders we set off by train, bus and snow buggy for Leivasbu in the middle of the Jotunheim Mountains. This is a remote and beautiful spot above the tree line. On returning from skiing the first day I received word that my father had died. As the snow buggy only made scheduled trips to Leivasbu once a week it was not feasible to get out and we were forced to remain in the mountains. We went on long ski trips during the days and enjoyed the Norwegian hospitality in the evenings. There were typical Norwegian delicacies such as reindeer, salmon and pickled herrings. Alcohol was limited on account of its high price. Liv and I danced quietly in the evenings with the sadness of my father's death hanging over our heads. Amongst the guests staying at the hotel were Harold and Margaret Barnes, marine biologists, who were working on the bibliography of a major scientific book they were writing. Every day they worked on their book in the mornings and went on long ski trips in the afternoons. I was to keep in touch with them for many years when they moved to the West coast of Scotland.

After our honeymoon in Norway I returned to Cornwall to console my Mother. My good friend Tim Evans had been most helpful and sympathetic in looking after my mother during my absence. Sadly I left my mother to return to Canada to resume my career and begin married life. Liv returned to work for the Norwegian Embassy. The season was a repeat of the first year with the first months spent in Lake Ontario and in July moving down the St Lawrence to work below Quebec. The typical problems of running a ship occurred, from dealing with drunken mates to incompetent cooks! The ship was based at Riviere du Loup during the week but on weekends we would normally go up river to Quebec City. This is a lovely and interesting city and Liv and I enjoyed the fine dining and ambiance whenever she would get down to visit the ship.

In mid July it was planned for the ship to spend a weekend in Quebec but unfortunately the radar had broken down and a technician was not available to repair it. As the persistent fog seemed to have cleared it was decided to attempt the trip without the radar. We were then based in Riviere du Loup and our first courses on this trip were to pass through the Hare Islands in mid channel and pick up the main shipping route on the north side of the river. Just as darkness was falling the fog returned. No sooner had this happened and *Cartier* was in the shipping channel off Malbaie (Murray Bay) when the lights of a large ship were seen closing rapidly. In spite of all efforts to go full stern on the engines *Cartier* was struck by the much larger oil tanker that disappeared into the fog, leaving all aboard my little ship much shaken! Fortunately the damage was all above the waterline and no water was taken aboard. One of the young trainees who had decided that hydrographic surveys were safer than land surveys where they spent a lot of time in helicopters quickly changed his mind. *Cartier* was not the only ship in trouble during that time and a very serious wreck and loss of crew had taken place during the same period. Following our encounter we anchored clear of the channel and inspected the damage. Fortunately there seemed to be no ingress of the sea and the main problem seemed to be some structural damage to the anchor windless and the bow in its vicinity. We decided to carry on up the river after the fog cleared to get the repair work done in Quebec City. By the end of July the damage had all been skilfully repaired by Davey Bros. Shipyard across the river from Quebec in Levis. The work included getting the radar operational again.

At the end of July we moved down the river again to resume our work and training programme. During part of the cruise the ship worked in the Saguenay River. This is a very deep fjord with high cliffs on each side. At the entrance is the small village of Tadoussac where I was to spend an entire summer some years later. Tadoussac was one of the first places where the French landed in Canada and established a religious outpost. Due to the turbulent water and strong currents it is much favoured by wild life, particularly in the form of the white beluga whales and other small whales. During August the weather had much improved and the fog had all gone. We took the ship down river into the open estuary to enable some training in oceanographic data collection. This was mainly in the area of Anticosti Island that I had visited some years before on the *Kapuskasing* surveys. We returned to the Saguenay River where we made some observations of the oceanography

In early September it was time to return up the St Lawrence Seaway to spend the last of the season in Lake Ontario. We worked in the eastern end of Lake Ontario in the vicinity of Amherst Island. Later in the month we de-commissioned for the winter once more in Kingston. It had been decided that it would be a good idea in October if office personnel were given the opportunity to spend a day on a survey ship. Accordingly, on several days, a bus full of the office staff, were driven from Ottawa to Kingston, where they boarded *Cartier*. At that time of year the leaves were changing colour and the scenery was beautiful. I took *Cartier* through the Thousand Islands at the start of the St Lawrence River where the ship could be taken through various narrow and interesting passages. The visitors were enthralled. The catering staff gave them a good lunch and they were put ashore and into the buses having spent a most enjoyable day. These trips were a great benefit to me because subsequently I was able to relate well to the purchasing department and other administrative units on a very friendly basis!

Once again I returned to the routine of working for the Ships' Division, this time with my old chief from *Baffin,* D'Arcy Charles, in charge. A change of work this year was to participate in a Government wide interview programme in which a recruiting team visited universities across Canada as part of its drive to employ engineers. I sometimes thought the students interviewed already knew more about the work than I did! On one occasion I was asked to give a lecture on hydrographic surveying to the Survey Engineering class at the University of New Brunswick and looking back I realised in retrospect, how ill equipped was my own education to lecture these students! A small incident during those lectures was to see a box full of the steel rings that Canadian professional engineers wear, sitting on the lecture podium, presumably to fit them to the fingers of the graduating engineers. It crossed my mind that I should slip a ring onto my own finger and become an immediate engineer!

For the 1964 survey season aboard *Cartier* it was decided that all training would be carried out aboard *Baffin* in the warm waters of the Caribbean. This left *Cartier* free to carry out a normal survey programme in the Great Lakes with fully trained surveyors aboard. Our task was to do a complete survey of Georgian Bay, a large offshoot from Lake Huron. A new electronic positioning system called Hi-Fix was to be used. This required transmitting stations to be set up at strategic points around the bay. The plan was for the centre part of the bay to be surveyed by the ship itself and various channels and ports around the periphery of the bay would be surveyed by the two launches that the ship carried. These launch parties would work as independent units from *Cartier* during the week but on alternate weekends would be visited by the ship to examine the data and pass it on for central processing. Georgian Bay has a beautiful coastline that has appeared in many of the paintings by the well known Canadian Group of Seven artists.[10] The water is clear and for most of the time reasonably calm. The launches working inshore at such places as Parry Sound, Owen Sound, the French River and Killarney were able to work most of the time in sheltered waters. There is a well sheltered route that follows most of the coastline of Georgian Bay that is very popular with recreational sailors during the summer months and one of our tasks was to thoroughly survey this route as a prelude to compiling navigational charts.

Liv and various friends visited *Cartier* on some of the weekends that the ship was accessible. Georgian Bay is a very popular resort area and there were many opportunities to swim and picnic. It was not always idyllic as I remember from a port visit to Lion Head on the west side of the bay. I was woken early in the morning by the local police force that needed me to keep my inebriated crew on board. I sent the crewman to his quarters with instructions not to come on deck until after we had sailed. When we did the policeman was still on the dock to ensure my drunken crew member did not return ashore. I also had difficulties with my own officers when my mate showed up to be a secret alcoholic.

---

[10] *A Vision of Canada*, The McMichael Collection.

After completing the survey of Georgian Bay I was instructed to go to Point Pelee that is located on the north west part of Lake Erie. This long finger of land stretches south into the lake but being comprised of fine sediments the nearby seafloor is continually changing. Each storm alters the shape of the point and the adjacent sub bottom. Point Pelee is well known as an assembly point for the large Monarch butterflies which gather on the point in preparation for making their way south across Lake Erie and down into the United States and on to Mexico From a commercial point of view the area is also known for growing tomatoes and a large Heinz plant dominates the local industry. With the Point Pelee survey completed it was time to move back to Kingston for the vessel's refit and a change in my career.

CHANGE OF CAREER

During the winter of 1963/64 various matters had been discussed in the Canadian Hydrographic Service. (CHS). As part of a major restructuring of the marine activities of the Government the CHS was absorbed in the newly formed Marine Sciences Branch. The politicians had decided to give greater attention to the oceans and particularly to oceanography. The ships became the common resource of both oceanographers and hydrographers. A new Director, Bill Cameron was appointed, a somewhat fearsome appearing man but an experienced and wise scientist. A major building programme was put into effect constructing large marine research stations on each coast to study the maritime area and at Burlington, near Toronto, to serve the Great Lakes. The first of these to be built was the Bedford Institute of Oceanography at Dartmouth, Nova Scotia. On formation of the new organisation eight of the middle level hydrographers, including myself, were interviewed for a managerial job in the new Atlantic Regional Centre. It came as a shock when we all failed the interview because of a lack of academic knowledge. This led to the University Training Plan in which selected hydrographic surveyors could attend university and be paid by the Government both their wages and the course fees. This was both shrewd and generous of the Canadian Government and was the start of a major drive to improve the academic knowledge of the hydrographic community. Several of the middle level hydrographers took up the programme and went to the Survey Engineering

Course at the University of New Brunswick.

I did not initially elect to take up the University Training Plan as another interesting programme was starting up and I wished to be involved. Computer technology was beginning to have a strong influence on both surveying and marine cartography. A large automatic plotting unit had been placed on the survey ship *Baffin* and was used for drawing the lattices required for plotting the new electronic positioning systems. Previously this time consuming work was done by hand. An important step was made when a Scottish academic, working at the University of Saskatchewan, Dr Ray Boyle, was contracted to carry out a study directed at introducing digital technology into the chart production. I was asked by my supervisors to become involved in this work as the project manager. In parallel with the University of Saskatchewan contract other types of technical development were beginning in all the regional offices and I became the coordinator of this ground breaking and interesting work. The problem of converting all the analogue data to digital data was central to much of this work. It was decided to send a group to visit European Hydrographic Offices to see how they were handling these matters. I was happily invited to join the group. This marked the start of my later developing interest in international marine matters. The group visited Sweden, Finland, Germany and the United Kingdom. It was evident that Canada had much to learn from them all, particularly Sweden. The Swedish chief hydrographer Dr Per Olaf Fagerholm took the opportunity of the Canadian visit, accompanied by some Americans, to show his national press how clever they were in Sweden and how rich North American countries were visiting Sweden to see their technology. The trip involved visits to some remote islands in the Baltic, such as Christian Oy, where the group were entertained at a reception by the lighthouse keeper. The different personalities of the Scandinavian countries were then evident such as the formality of the Swedes and the friendliness of the Danes. We visited a paper company in Finland and enjoyed their formal hospitality but then went on to Sweden to find they were upset that we thought the Finns were more formal than they were. We did not at that time visit Norway, which later became a leader in the new hydrographic technology.

On returning to Canada the task was to put some of the technology that we had seen in Europe into action. An engineering colleague, Tim Evangelatos and I developed a software package called HYPOS (Hydrographic Positioning System) that provided a semi-manual method of converting analogue soundings into digital form and merging them with the geographic positions. Our paper on HYPOS was the first that I had written and was published in the International Hydrographic Review.[11] It was the first of many technical papers that I was to write and have published during my career.

In the summer of 1964 I persuaded my managers that a major survey should be set up to test and evaluate some of

---

[11] AJ Kerr, *Hypos – A System for Processing Hydrographic Survey Data*, Int Hydrographic Review Vol XLVI No 2, 1969

the new technology. It was decided that the survey base was to be in Tadoussac on the St Lawrence River which I had first visited and knew from my time on *Cartier* .The previous autumn I visited the area to establish the basic geographic control and investigate domestic arrangements for the large survey crew. I was assisted by a rather flamboyant surveyor called Joe McCarthy, who later had much to contribute to both the work and to the social affairs. A deal was struck to accommodate the crew in the Tadoussac Hotel. This was one of several fine hotels that had been built by the railway company Canadian Pacific, as a stopping point for their ships that carried passengers down the St Lawrence River from Montreal and up the Saguenay River to Chicoutimi. The business had run down and the hotels been sold off. The present owners were only too happy to provide accommodation for a Government survey team. During the early spring of 1964 the survey took its fleet of high speed survey launches down the river from Quebec. It was really too early in the year and a hard trip but eventually the fleet was established alongside the quay in Tadoussac with offices set up in trailers nearby. One of the numerous small problems to sort out was the Bishop of Chicoutimi complaining to our Government minister that a number of signs had been set up by our surveyors on one of his retreats at the entrance to the Saguenay River. These signs warned people of the danger of high electricity voltage. In fact it was a message to keep people away from the transmitting antennae used for positioning the survey. The matter was soon resolved by Joe McCarthy, a Roman Catholic himself, going to the retreat with some small financial compensation for the Bishop's flock

The survey was demanding, both technically and socially. The fleet of survey launches ranged across the St Lawrence River as far as Rimouski on the south shore. The launches were fast, travelling at speeds of over 25 knots and were continuously positioned by the electronic system Hi-Fix. Miles of survey data were gathered. A side wall hovercraft owned by the Decca company in the United Kingdom, called SURVEYMARINE, was to be evaluated. Unlike most hovercraft that have a skirt all around to hold the air cushion on which the vehicle was supported, the side wall version had solid keels on each side with skirts at the forward and aft ends. The system was fast and manoeuvrable when it operated but the considerable amount of flotsam in the river damaged the skirts. It had an innovative navigation and control system, and could be set to run in a hands off mode of surveying a pattern of parallel tracks. Although it was later used in different parts of the World its vulnerability to the flotsam found in many Canadian waters rendered it unacceptable for surveys of those waters. My old colleague from Arctic days, Ross Douglas was brought up from the Atlantic Region for trials of a new digital sounding and logging system on a launch called *Dunlin.* This was to be the start of high speed digital data collection.

Socially the survey crew was well entertained by the fact that many of the hotel staff were attractive young female university students from Laval University in Quebec. On Saturdays there was always a grand fete in the village. Young students came down to Tadoussac to ski down the steep sand hills and into the river. The experimental survey operation resulted in visits from management staff from Ottawa Headquarters and other regional offices. One of my memories is of a visit from the rather stern Director of the Atlantic Region, Russ Melanson, who was a keen trout fisherman. The hotel had some trout lakes and I had arranged to take him fishing in one of the hotel's boats. Unfortunately, on my back cast my fly caught my guest on the lip. Fortunately the hook was not well embedded. Another memory was when the party was visited by the Dominion Hydrographer. The drunken crew of the hovercraft telephoned him in the middle of the night to ask if he wanted to buy a battleship. He was not amused.

The survey, unhappily put a great strain on my relationship with Liv. She had decided to spend a large part of the summer in Norway and I was left to my own devices, including some female relationships and the care of our pure bred dogs which established friendships with the local mongrels. Tadoussac was then a place of two identities or Two Solitudes as Hugh McLennan had called them in his 1945 book. In the village was the local French Canadian community but overlooking the bay was a row of fine large houses that were summer homes for wealthy people from Quebec and Montreal. These included both French and English Canadians. Amongst them was the George Vanier family. From 1959 – 1967 he was the first nationally born Governor General of Canada. Apart from a friendship that I struck up with the Price family, who were large land owners and timber merchants, who lived during the summer in the old Tadoussac pilot house, the surveyors had very little to do with the summer visitors but intermingled freely with the villagers, in spite of the language difficulties. In October the weather deteriorated and the survey closed down with the fleet of launches being taken for the winter to the Coast Guard base at Quebec and the surveyors returning to Ottawa. During the long summer the main objectives of the project had been met and we had been able to evaluate much of the new digital technology used for collecting and processing the data. At the same time we had systematically surveyed a large area of the St Lawrence River.

University Training Plan

I had seen the need for university qualifications soon after arriving in Canada. I had struggled to gain entry to university by studying via the Department of Veteran's Affairs correspondence course. This had eventually led to my gaining senior matriculation qualifications in the required subjects. Some of my colleagues, including Mike Eaton, had already been on the University Training Plan and I felt that it was time to apply myself. I had been taking evening courses in mathematics at Carleton University but now felt that I should undertake a course that was more directly relevant to my present work interests, namely Computer Science. In retrospect this was a mistake because the technology was changing so rapidly that everything I had been taught became quickly obsolete. It would have been far better if I had continued with my studies in mathematics. Computer Science was at the time being offered by the University of Ottawa. This was a French speaking university and I thought an added advantage would be to improve my rusty French. As it turned out many of the students also needed support with the French language and many of the course notes were provided in both English and French.

Becoming a full time university student for the first time at the age of 33 seemed rather old but I now realise that today many people enrol even later. One thing in my favour was that I knew what I was looking for in the way of knowledge and I found that along with some of my other hydrographic colleagues we did well in our studies. Although much of the computer science subjects quickly became obsolete I was very pleased with some of the pure engineering subjects, particularly electrical engineering. Due to my concern for possibly losing my place in the career ladder I had decided not to put in the extra year required to get an honours degree and was thrilled when I graduated to find I was on the Dean's Honour List.

During my time at the University of Ottawa Liv and I lived in South Ottawa. As both our house and the university were beside the Rideau Canal that was frozen and made into a skating rink during the winter I was able to ski to work every day along the snowy verge that surrounded the icy surface of the ice rink. I hid my skis in a drainpipe in the wall of the canal and walked across the road to the university. It was a busy time of studying for both Liv and myself. She had decided to study part time for a course in Mediterranean history and was also deep into the books every evening. Our downstairs neighbours during that time were Professor Emery and Sharon Fortin. He was a French Canadian from Chicoutimi and pretended to strongly support the Quebec cause, though I believe that he enjoyed living in the mainly Anglophone city of Ottawa. Over the years since we have amused ourselves at Christmas time by sending each other cards which said rude things about the Reine de l'Angleterre or le President de Gaulle. Emery was a determined trout fisherman and he and I spent many happy weekends chasing the plentiful brook trout in the adjacent Province of Quebec. I would tease him that the Brook trout in those lakes were not nearly as clever as the brown trout which existed in English waters. During the years at university I was initially involved in processing the mountain of data from the Tadoussac survey. Later I was given a staff role in the research and development work.

REGIONAL HYDROGRAPHER – CENTRAL REGION

As part of the structuring of the Marine Sciences the Hydrographic Service became divided into three Regional offices and a Headquarters in Ottawa. The regional hydrographic units worked under the general umbrella of the Marine Sciences Regions across the width of Canada. Each of the separate regional hydrographic groups was managed by a senior hydrographer who later held the title of Regional Director. Shortly after I graduated from the University of Ottawa the job of Regional Hydrographer for the Central Region located at the new Canada Centre for Inland Waters (CCIW), became vacant. This large centre was located at Burlington, Ontario, not far from Toronto. Overall the Centre was managed by Tom McCulloch, a tough Scot. I was appointed to the job in early 1972. Up to that time I had strenuously resisted a move to the regions but the job in Burlington seemed a good career direction. However the transfer out of Ottawa was not favoured by Liv who enjoyed living in that city and her job at the Norwegian Embassy. We moved into a period of uncertainty but eventually I made the firm decision to move and that was the end of our ten years of marriage. No doubt, while the decision to move to Burlington was the final move our marriage had been rocky for some time mainly because we were both actively pursuing our own professional interests. After parting company Liv went on to join the Norwegian Foreign Service and become a diplomat. Eventually she rose to the dizzy heights of Norway's Ambassador to Brazil.

I much enjoyed my working life in Burlington. Tom McCulloch was a great man to work for. He stood no truck from those administrative persons, such as personnel and finance officers, whom he considered worked for him and not vice versa. He was happy to have me lead the hydrographic programme and above all he was successful in seeing that my programme was well funded. The geographic area of work was huge extending from Lake Winnipeg in the west to the Gulf of St Lawrence in the east. It also included the whole of Hudson Bay to the north. I had a good team and amongst them was Rick Bryant, a development engineer who subsequently became Director of the Pacific Coast Guard. He and his wife Nancy became great friends. Another engineer Don Knudsen was also on my staff and later went on with his wife to run a successful acoustic engineering business.

My domestic arrangements needed some sorting out. Once it had been determined that Liv was not joining me I had to find a permanent residence. My secretary found me a small house on the lakeshore at Stoney Creek on the outskirts of Hamilton. This was part of a larger property owned by Watson and June Wright, Canadians of Irish descent who owned and managed some local engineering business. They were very happy to have me move in beside them. They were very social and enjoyed having a younger person to share the fun. It was a pretty location with vineyards behind separating the house from the industrial city of Hamilton. In front the grass lawn stretched down to the shore of Lake Ontario. Hamilton is the site of a heavy steel making industry. The air and the lake water were both quite polluted but the particles in the air caused the most wonderful red sunsets. During the winter Lake Ontario froze and in the process created a high berm of ice all along the shore. In the summer this all disappeared and the water was clear and warm enough for swimming. I bought a small yacht, which I renamed *Cornish Chough* that I moored in Hamilton Bay. During the summer when the weather was calmer I moved the boat to a mooring just off the house at Stoney Creek. This ended up in disaster on one occasion when during a sudden summer storm the boat dragged its mooring and ended up on the shingle beach in front of the house. Fortunately the boat was not seriously damaged and I had a Cornish friend, John Lomas, who worked as a rigger for the research station and also had access to a crane truck which he used to rescue the boat. My office at the Canada Centre for Inland Waters faced onto the channel leading in and out of Hamilton Bay. The large lake carriers, loaded with iron ore on their way to the steel plant, passed right in front of my window.

While the business of managing the regional hydrographic office was demanding and involved many trips over the Regional area, a matter had arisen that was to influence me much in the future. During 1972 and prior to my move to Burlington, Ottawa was the site of two large international scientific meetings. These were organised by the International Geographical Union (IGU) and the International Cartographic Association (ICA). I had been asked to provide a site at my small farm in the Gatineau for a large picnic associated with these conferences. This provided a great thrill for the people of many nationalities that were participating. However a more lasting importance to my future career was to be nominated by an American naval captain, Victor Moitoret, to become the future chair of ICA's Commission on Marine Cartography. Commissions of these large scientific organisations have considerable power in arranging the scientific agenda. They normally met every four or five years, usually in some distant and exotic land and this required the arrangement of the presentation of papers and workshops. In 1975 I actively participated in the ICA Conference in Moscow as Chairman of the Marine Cartography Commission. At that time the Iron Curtain was in place and there was considerable security involved. I was interviewed by the RCMP (Royal Canadian Mounted Police) both before and after his visit and thoroughly briefed on what to do and what not to do. On arrival in Moscow I was met by two carers, a young man and an attractive young lady. They arranged all my moves and took me to see such attractions as the Moscow Circus and Le Fleidermaus – or flying bat as my guide called it. Chairmen of Commissions of international organisations were very well treated and respected in the Soviet Union. I recall a trip on a tour boat in the canals near Moscow. While my fellow chairmen and I enjoyed champagne and caviar in a warm cabin, the rest of the conference attendees milled about the deck in the cold! Through my work with the ICA I came in close contact with the International Hydrographic Organisation (IHO), which was going to have a great influence on my future life. In particular the IHO was involved in updating a major chart series covering all the World's Oceans, called the General Bathymetric Chart of the Oceans (GEBCO).[12] There was considerable debate at the time between the hydrographers and oceanographers on how the data should be presented with the more traditionally minded hydrographers wanting a display similar to navigational charts and the oceanographers and other scientists wanting a more interpretive display. The IHO and the ICA , as well as the Intergovernmental Commission (IOC) of UNESCO were involved.

After my move to Burlington and my separation from Liv, I led a busy life of enjoyment with the fair sex but this all steadied up when I was introduced by my landlord's family to Judith, who worked as a nurse at the Hamilton General Hospital. Over a period Judith and Leslie, her six year old daughter, came to share my life. We lived together in the small house by the lake and saw much of Watson and June. There were many sailing trips on Lake Ontario, often with friends Rick and Nancy Bryant. There were trips away from Stoney Creek, such as fishing for large trout and salmon on Manitoulin Island. Burlington was distant from the ski slopes but trips were arranged both in Canada and across to Europe. In 1977 I was invited to the International Hydrographic Conference in Monaco as an observer for the ICA . It was decided that Judith would accompany me and

---

[12] *The History of GEBCO 1903-2003.*

that also we would combine it with a ski holiday in Ischgl, Austria and also with a sailing adventure in the United Kingdom. This was my first attendance at a series of conferences of the IHO, which are regularly arranged every five years.

Figure 30 Here is Judith on the *A-OH-HA*. She is standing in front of the Aries Vane Steering Gear. At the end of the Monaco trip, we took the boat to Ireland. We sailed from Cornwall to Waterford and along the south coast of Ireland to Glengarrif before laying up.

Prior to the IH Conference another development had taken place. Responding to an advertisement in the Toronto Globe & Mail I had bought unseen the *A-OH-HA*, a 30 foot yacht. Initially I had thought that it was for sale in Dartmouth, Nova Scotia but it turned out that it was in fact in Dartmouth, UK. The problem was how to get the boat to Canada. At that time returning Canadian residents, who had spent some years overseas, could bring in returning settlers effects, such as cars, without paying the import tax, which amounted to around 30% of the value. As I was trying to convince my managers that I should spend a year at the IHO on a secondment I had hoped to take advantage of the tax loophole bringing the boat to Canada on my return. However my assignment to the IHO had yet to materialise and I now owned a boat in the United Kingdom and had to avoid paying the large tax on entry to Canada.

The IH Conference in Monaco was a great eye opener for me into the world of international hydrography. Hydrographic ships from several countries visited the port and there were many receptions and other social occasions. The delegates discussed international standards, technology transfer and much else that would lead to improved marine navigation. Canada, with its emphasis on new technology was much respected, if considered a bit brash, by some of the larger well established hydrographic offices in the UK and USA.

On return to Burlington my proposals that I should become even more involved in international marine matters were beginning to be considered. At that time the Canadian Government was giving increased attention to Francophone interests and bilingualism. All senior staff positions in the Government were expected to be bilingual and to help achieve that end French immersion classes were being offered. These courses were only marginally successful. Many of the Anglophone civil servants, including myself, were not totally convinced of the new policies. I was more concerned in promoting my career in hydrography than of spending many months in a classroom learning French. I suggested to my managers that I might be seconded to the International Hydrographic Bureau, the Secretariat of the IHO in Monaco, where I could continue with my hydrographic work and at the same time work in a French speaking environment. Before this idea was agreed it was then proposed to me that I explore other options. By that time the need to become fluent in French had become secondary to the idea of greater involvement in international marine affairs. The University of Rhode Island in the USA and the University of Wales both offered interesting master's degrees in marine science law and policy. I proposed to my superiors that I should apply to the University of Wales and that was accepted both by the university and my superiors.

Before the plans to attend the University of Wales were put into place there remained the matter of getting *A-OH-HA* to Canada. It was decided to sail the boat across the Atlantic. Aware of the difficulties of sailing a small 30 foot boat across the Atlantic I sought the help of an old friend of my father's, Michael Ritchie, who was the Director of the Royal Institute of Navigation. He was an excellent navigator and had sailed in the Single Handed Trans Atlantic race many times. Mike was to become a great friend and advisor. His own trips across the Atlantic had been in the even smaller 26 foot folk boat *Jester*. He advised me to start as early in the year as possible, ideally in May, to avoid the development of hurricanes later in the summer. He suggested that there were essentially three courses: The Trade Wind route, which involved going down to the Canary Islands, across to the Caribbean and up the American coast. This is a long route of over 5000 nautical miles but generally enjoys favourable winds and warm weather; then there is the *on the nose* route, which means following the great circle or possibly the rhumbline route straight across the North Atlantic. This includes a strong probability of tacking against head winds and passes through the cold weather and contrary currents of the Grand Banks. The route is however much shorter and is approximately 2,500 miles in length; Finally there is the intermediate route, favoured by multi hulls, that goes through the Azores and then due west and across the Gulf Stream to the American coast This route is typically about 3,500 miles and was the route I chose for *A-OH-HA*.

In my crew were two other hydrographers, Derek Cooper and James Bruce. Judith had originally thought to make the trip but had not got on well with Derek Cooper who had sailed with us in Ireland the previous year. I thoroughly enjoyed oceanic cruising because of the great variety of conditions to be considered. Storms had to be faced and favourable winds enjoyed. *A-OH-HA* , although small, proved to be a seaworthy little vessel. An automatic steering device, called an Aries Wind Vane, helped considerably with keeping the boat on course. We stopped at Horta in the Azores, where *A-OH-HA*'s name was painted on the dock wall perpetuating the tradition of many yachts. The first leg of the trip from Mousehole in Cornwall took 11 days and then another 25 days on to Newport, Rhode Island. At Newport my of leave had run out and I had arranged for another crew to take the boat to New York and up the Hudson River to Lake Ontario. I had planned to take the boat across to Burlington but problems with the Canadian Customs concerning the registered ownership of the boat led to the rest of the summer keeping the boat in American waters operating out of the Niagara River in the small port of Lewiston. This was a pleasantly busy little American town. Navigation on the river was particularly difficult due to the irregular eddies of water that came down from the Niagara Falls. In September it was time to go over to Wales to enrol in the university. *A-OH-HA* had to be taken into Canadian waters and placed under the care of the Customs Authorities until I could sort out the problems of import tax.

For me the University of Wales assignment had materialised and now married to Judith, accompanied by her daughter Leslie, we were off to Cardiff, Wales, in time to start the university year in September 1977. Once again I appreciated the generosity of the Canadian Government in agreeing to continue to pay my wages, a living allowance and the university fees.

UNIVERSITY OF WALES

My new family and I were able to find a small modern house in Radyr, a suburb of Cardiff. Leslie, a young teenager, was enrolled in a local comprehensive school. Not only did she have to adapt to a totally new school system but was aghast to find she had to learn Welsh. For my own studies the course for a Master's degree in Marine Law and Policy lasted a year for those for whom English was a mother tongue and two years for those that needed additional help with English, many of these being North Africans with marine qualifications. The course had three elements: a background of economic developments in the oceans, such as the offshore oil industry and fishing that was run by the Department of Marine Geography; Admiralty Law provided by the Legal Department, which mainly provided examples of matters such as marine insurance and salvage; and International Law of the Sea, also provided by the legal department. I found all of the elements of the course useful and of direct application to my interests, particularly the international law. The professors were entertaining and knowledgeable. Professor Cadwallader, kept us enthralled with stories of false claims to salvage. He also entertained us by taking us to watch the seven a sides and other rugby in Cardiff Arms Park and at Lampeter, West Wales. My driving interest was in International marine law, mainly taught by Professor EB Brown. Interestingly I recall that he had published a paper that asked the rhetorical question of 'Scotland's Oil?' I was cynical about the claims of international law, viewing it more as a power play than actual law. I have always held the opinion that in many cases international lawyers identify political solutions and then looked for precedents that support the case. I was much taken up by the subject of maritime boundary delimitation. This was to have considerable effect on my later career interests. My dissertation was an analysis of the Anglo-French Continental Shelf arbitration. This delimitation was influenced by the complicated sovereignty and geographic disposition of the Channel Islands. The status of islands have long presented difficulties in maritime boundary law as I was discover myself in cases in which I was later involved.

Taking the course with me was another Canadian, Jack Buchan, from Vancouver. He was a practising lawyer and was attending the course to strengthen his knowledge in marine matters. Jack and his wife Nancy became great friends with Judith and I. During the time at the University of Wales we developed a group of acquaintances in Cardiff and at nearby Brecon, where my old friend Tim Evans and his wife Jill were living. Tim was a local agricultural advisor. In Cardiff we got to know a fellow Cornishman, Russell Greenslade and his American wife Susie. Russell taught textile design at a local art school but after I had finished my course they emigrated to the USA on the same ship as we did. Some other people known during that time were David and Allison Bickmore, who although living near Oxford they came down regularly to an old hill farm they owned at Capel y Fin. David was an expert cartographer, who introduced the new digital mapping technology to the Experimental

Cartography Unit at the Royal College of Art.

An exciting and most important event for Judith and I while living in Wales was the birth of our first son Andrew at the Cardiff University Hospital. Attendance at the University of Wales also allowed my family to see something of my elderly mother in Cornwall and to generally spend much time in the West Country. She was thrilled to see her first grandchild. During the winter we experienced an unusually hostile winter with unusually heavy snow falls. Christmas and the New Year were spent in Cornwall. On completion of the course work we returned to Cornwall to write up the required dissertation. In the final results for the course my Canadian friend, Jack Buchan, came first and I second, a very satisfactory conclusion to my time at the University of Wales. When the time came to return to Canada we decided that we should return with all our belongings by sea. There were limited opportunities but we were able to secure accommodation on the Russian liner *Alexander Pushkin.* This was a far cry from the magnificent Cunard liner *Ivernia* on which I had originally gone to Canada. A particular problem on that trip was looking after Andrew, our young son. By Western standards the stewarding staff had rather primitive ideas of how to look after a baby, stating that they were engineers and not nursemaids! However after a rather stormy September crossing I once again arrived at Montreal by ship and to return to a job in Ottawa.

RETURN TO OTTAWA

My agreement on going to university had been that I should vacate my office as Director of the Central Region. When I returned it was to work as a staff officer in Ottawa. We found an old farm house, once more in the Gatineau Hills and settled down to the life of an Ottawa civil servant. Fortunately a nucleus of my old friends remained and they took well to Judith. Ragnar, Colin and Linda Bergh and many of my old Scandinavian friends remained and the parties and good life were re-vitalised. The house was in the centre of the Hills with cross country ski trails going directly from our doorstep. Our son Andrew was carried for many miles in a rucksack along the ski trails. The cold was intense and for a period of two months the water supply, which came from a well about 50 metres from the house was solidly frozen. When the thaw did come the basement flooded and we spent a night bailing out water to prevent the furnace from being submerged.

At the office I had a staff role concerning a special Arctic project. I did not think highly of Gerry Ewing, who was then the Dominion Hydrographer. He was a geophysicist and had been given credit for the Canadian support of the GEBCO (General Bathymetric Chart of the Oceans) programme that I felt was really not his making.

Nova Scotia and the Bedford Institute

In 1980 during a reorganisation of the senior hydrographic staff I was appointed the Director of the Atlantic Region of the Hydrographic Service. This was based at the Bedford Institute in Dartmouth. It was a demanding and interesting job involving considerable interaction with the scientists working in the whole range of marine science activities. Originally I had strongly resisted a move to Nova Scotia but others, including Mike Eaton, had moved there years before and had thrived and in retrospect it was to provide some of my best times in Canada.

We bought a house in Glen Margaret, about 20 miles south of Halifax and on an inlet of the sea. It was of wooden clap board and of a type called a Captain's House, being quite old for the area and built in the eighteenth century. Taking up the appointment at BIO(Bedford Institute of Oceanography) provided an opportunity for another sailing adventure. *A-OH-HA* had to be moved from the Great Lakes to Nova Scotia. This trip takes you down the St Lawrence Seaway and across the Gulf of St Lawrence. You then go through the Straits of Canso, that separate Cape Breton Island from the rest of Nova Scotia and from there it is a run along the rugged Nova Scotia coast to Halifax. Judith and I and our very young son Andrew made the trip. It was a long and at times rough voyage but a great way for me to take up my new job. On the first day of our trip, while motoring down the St Lawrence River Andrew fell overboard but very fortunately was lifted aboard again on his harness. A sadness of the trip was to lose our golden retriever that was run over on a stop at Rimouski. We were fortunate in being able to sell our old farm house in the Gatineau during the trip and so could move our possessions directly into the house at Glen Margaret and have *A-OH-HA* moored in the bay opposite it. The main problem of the house, we realised afterwards, was that the commute into work each day for both of us was long and perilous when the roads became icy in the winter.

Work at the Bedford Institute was demanding and fascinating. It was in a large scientific establishment with programmes going on in a great variety of disciplines of marine sciences. All of these shared the resources of the Institute and in particular the ships which were part of the resources. This involved ongoing negotiations to share the ships, some of which got very heated. *Baffin* was by then getting quite old and undergoing a mid-life refit. This was designed to make the ship equally capable to carry out hydrography and scientific research. Another large ship *Hudson,* designed specifically for oceanographic research had been built. The closest discipline to hydrography was that of the Atlantic Geoscience Centre that was then managed by Mike Keen, with whom I got on well. Bosco Loncarevic was another geologist with whom I had had a long relationship and he was a great supporter of hydrography. Reg Gilbert, who originally came to the Institute from Cambridge University, as did several of the other scientists, had taken charge of all the facilities and ensuring hydrography had its fair share always involved a struggle. The Director General, Alan Longhurst was a marine biologist and tried to keep the competing interests happy. I remember that when I claimed that something was not fair Alan Longhurst would say that life was not fair and everything had to be negotiated. During my time at the Institute the political demands of the fishing industry strengthened and in the end the Institute included a large element of fisheries research. Another political pressure was to develop capability in Canadian industry to develop equipment for marine science. To this end the Institute campus had commercial units added so that government scientists could work side by side with commercial companies. This move was to prove rewarding in developing Canadian expertise that could be sold internationally. An engineer who had left the BIO staff to form a small engineering company was John Brooke, He and his wife Mary were great friends.

In the Regional Hydrographic Office there was an active field programme that involved surveys spread throughout all the Atlantic Provinces and much of the Eastern Arctic. Some of the field activities were based on ships and other used launches from shore stations. The Bay of Fundy was in the domain of my responsibility and with the largest tides in the World it provided an active field for research. My assistant, Bert Smith, was a tough Nova Scotian who kept the survey part of the programme under strict control. He had experienced all the hard rigours in the field himself and expected all the surveyors to live in the same way. I recall that when one of the surveyors wanted some leave from the surveys to be present for the birth of a child he got short shrift from Bert who said that he had never himself been able to get out of the field for such a purpose.

During the years that I managed the regional office it was decided to have much greater decentralisation of all the hydrographic activities. While to date all the survey work was carried out in the regional offices the chart production, with the exception of the Pacific Coast, had been mainly based in Ottawa. It was decided that all chart production was to be moved from the Ottawa Headquarters to the regions as well. This was met with strong resistance from many of the cartographers who were much less accustomed to separation from their roots than were the field surveyors. Never the less during my time at the Institute almost all of the chart production for the Atlantic provinces was moved to the Bedford Institute. Compounding the difficulties was a change to make much use of digital technology. Research into navigation and positioning was critical not only for hydrography but for many other forms of marine science. During the years since the positioning system Loran C had been first introduced in the nineteen fifties there had been much active research to understand the propagation of the signals and to generally ensure the accuracy of observations using the technology. When satellite technology came into being, first through Doppler measurements and later in the form of the Global Positioning System (GPS) the navigational research continued. Much of this work was overseen by Mike Eaton, who was joined by Dave Wells, who later established a link with the Department of Survey Engineering at the University of New Brunswick. During the time I was associated with the Institute the Navigational Research group began to become greatly involved in new digital cartographic technology. A system was developed at the University of New Brunswick called CARIS and the Canadian Hydrographic Service established an international reputation in the development and use of the digital technology. A particularly fascinating area of technical research taking place during my years at the Institute was the development of robotic craft. This was largely due to the initiative of Reg Gilbert but the actual developments took place at International Submarine Engineering (ISE), an engineering company in British Columbia. One of these vehicles was designed to accompany a large parent vessel to multiply its data collection ability. The vessel was called *Dolphin* and was essentially a torpedo shaped vessel 7 metres in length that travelled just beneath the surface. Re-fuelling the vessels at sea and recovering them in rough weather were just some of the difficulties that had to be faced. Another robotic craft was designed for work in ice covered waters and called *ARCS.* It was slightly smaller than the *Dolphin,* at about 6 metres, but more sophisticated. It was designed to travel beneath solid ice cover and was powered by nickel cadmium batteries. Clever acoustic technology was used to navigate under the ice and in particular to ensure that the submersible did not collide with keels protruding down from the ice. During my association with the project the development moved as far as test runs under water but not under ice. Some time after I left the Institute the funds from the Canadian Government dried up and the technology was bought by US Naval interests. Today there is a great interest in using robotic craft to sample both the depth and what is within the sea. Canada was very much in the lead in developing the technology.

It may be well asked how Canadian Government scientists obtained the funding to develop this very expensive technology. Regular resources available to Government Departments had been seriously reduced over the years but in order to encourage programmes directed at special political interests such as the environment and the Arctic funds were available. Much of my work involved *fishing* for funds available for these priorities. Fortunately in this activity my old colleague of Arctic days, Neil Anderson, worked with me at the Ottawa end and was very successful in finding money. So in spite of dwindling general resources several projects were supported by these special funds. In commenting on this strategy of acquiring Government funds the successful cooperation between the Canadian Hydrographic Service, the Department of Survey Engineering at the University of New Brunswick and the commercial company CARIS is worth noting. As far back as the 1960s the Canadian Government had encouraged the development of the Department of Survey Engineering. Lecturers had been provided and students supported. A strong link developed between the university and the Bedford Institute. One of the university professors, Dr Sam Masry, left to set up CARIS. The development of the software CARIS was to play an important part in placing Canadian cartographers and hydrographers in the international fore front of digital cartography.

As with my term at Burlington earlier my time at the Bedford Institute was not all work and no play. Halifax had changed greatly from the dour city of the post war years. There was considerable social interaction with my colleagues at the Institute both in the Hydrographic Service and with the scientists working there. With *A-OH-HA* now at hand there was excellent sailing in local waters, although the presence of fog in the early part of the summer made this challenging. Ongoing difficulties with the ownership of the boat led to the decision that the only way to resolve the tax matter was to sail it back to the United Kingdom and sell it in the UK. It was therefore decided in 1981 to take some time to sail the boat back across the Atlantic. A crew consisting of

Figure 31 *A-OH-HA* Crew in Mousehole.

my close friends Roger Morris, Tim Evans and Jim Bruce, were mustered to make the passage. With the prevailing winds more favourable than on the outward journey the return voyage took only 23 days. It was a remarkably good trip with the expected mixture of fine weather and gales. The crew that had mostly grown up together got on very well. A land fall was made in the Scilly Isles and later the yacht was returned and sold in Falmouth from where it had sailed over five years before.

Returning to Nova Scotia, our second son Timothy was born at the Halifax General Hospital. Judith and I decided that we should move closer to Halifax and reduce the commuting time. We found a half completed house near Prospect, about 15 miles from Halifax. The house was on a small peninsula comprised by a drumlin that had been connected to the mainland. It was approximately a third of an acre, surrounded by the sea on three sides. Its actual location was at the head of Prospect Bay, a long inlet of the sea. During the winter the sea in the bay opposite the house froze but in the summer it was warm enough for swimming. Ospreys flew overhead and otters and mink drifted back and forth with the ice or swam past during the summer. When we bought the house it was only half finished and we set to work to complete it by adding two bedrooms and a large living room. The construction was entirely of wood and the exterior was of cedar shingles. Having never built a house before it was an uphill learning process. It was magnificently situated with large windows looking up and down the inlet. It was quite close to the sea at high tide and in gales there was some concern that it might be swamped. It was heated by two large wood stoves and one of the tasks each year was to saw and split a mountain of firewood for the winter supply. The water supply was also a major consideration. The house itself was located on a drumlin which was simply a hillock of shingle and sand and did not provide a source of ground water. Instead the well had to be located on the adjacent mainland and was then pumped up in the well and down the hill to the house. In the winter snow clearing was paramount and as the house was on a private road it had to be dealt with by the community.

Figure 32 Our house on Prospect Bay, Nova Scotia.

Boats were still a large feature of our recreation. *A-OH-HA* had been sold in the United Kingdom and a St Pierre dory took its place. This was a 22 foot open boat that was of a design of those used on the French islands of St Pierre et Miquelin. It had been originally built for a salty old German,

Nils Jannasch, who had sailed on square riggers and was the Director of the Maritime Museum in Halifax. His parents had been missionaries on the Labrador coast and Nils had designed the boat with the idea of sailing up the Labrador coast but had never achieved that ambition. To cope with the pack ice it was sheathed in greenheart and was a great boat for our young sons and equipped with a simple diesel engine and a lug sail. The family used it for fishing and picnicking. Fishing was excellent in the inlet and off the nearby coast with many cod, haddock and mackerel. There was also a thriving stock of lobsters but strict rules restricted the catching of these to commercial fishermen. There were however shell fish in abundance with mussels growing on the beach on our doorstep and being grown commercially nearby. An Indian reservation on Cape Breton Island raised oysters and these could be purchased cheaply and then kept at hand off our own wharf. Nova Scotia is well known for its schooners, the most famous being the very large *Bluenose* that appears on Canadian coins.

One day we saw a very pretty little schooner, called *Sybarite*, at a marina on the Le Have River and ended up as its owners. It was only 30 feet in length but it had the traditional schooner rig with two masts and a fisherman's sail that was hoisted between the masts. *Sybarite* gave the family a much greater range of cruising and we joined the Nova Scotia Schooner Association. This was a hard sailing and hard drinking group that sailed and raced regularly along the Nova Scotia coast. *Sybarite* joined in with the racing and partying but was too small to be very competitive.

Figure 33 ***Sybarite*****.**

Our family had an idyllic time living on Prospect Bay. A Dinner Club gave a local social basis with other surveyors living in the area and with their mainly school teacher spouses. The boys originally went to the local grade school in Prospect but later were enrolled at a Convent school in Halifax where they were able to have some exposure to French. Judith worked as a nurse in the Operating Room at the Children's Hospital in Halifax, from which she had many tales of temperamental surgeons and of searches for lost needles during operations. I commuted regularly to the Bedford Institute when I was not travelling to meetings across Canada and occasionally abroad. During this period I became increasingly involved in the international activities of the International Cartographic Association (ICA) and the International Hydrographic Organisation (IHO).

Figure 34 The yellow *St Piere Dory* with two little naked boys in front.

A MOVE TO MONACO

Internationally, the work of the national Hydrographic Offices was brought together by the International Hydrographic Organisation (IHO). This organisation had its headquarters at Monaco as a result of the generosity of Prince Albert l in 1921. The Prince was most interested in oceanography and would take his large motor yacht out into the oceans to collect specimens to study. When the IHO was formed he had kindly offered to build premises for the IHO beside the harbour. Although over shadowed by the large Musee Oceanographique that was built on the Rock near the Palace the IHO counts itself very fortunate in being provided with its magnificent office to house its secretariat, called the International Hydrographic Bureau (IHB). The constitution required that the organisation be managed by a Directing Committee of three senior hydrographers elected every five years. During my time the overall staff of the IHB amounted to 18 people. These were mainly either French or Monagesque. The Directing Committee was elected from all the Member States of the organisation composed of many nationalities

While I was working in Nova Scotia the Canadian Hydrographic Service had become increasingly involved in supporting the IHO and was represented on several of its working groups and committees. Canadian hydrography had established an excellent position as being progressive and creative in terms of new technology. Canada decided that it would field a candidate for the elections that were to be held in 1987 and I was put forward for a post. The Directors, to that time, were generally senior naval officers of at least Captain's rank and frequently were Admirals. Although having had considerable experience in the Merchant shipping sector and in hydrography, I was a civilian. The election for the Directing Committee is a key event of the International Hydrographic Conferences. These conferences frequently support a candidate for election by sending their survey ships to Monaco during the Conferences and to use them as a base for providing receptions and showing off their national technology. There was also unofficial entertaining which took place at Rosie's Bar a rather unassuming place close to the Casino. It was said that more Admirals made more important decisions in Rosie's Bar than in the conference hall. It was also a meeting place for the engineers and drivers during the Annual Grand Prix. The walls and ceilings were covered in signatures of racing drivers and admirals from around the world. I had by then attended the five year conferences in 1977, 1982 and 1987 and was familiar with the procedures. In pursuit of one of my particular interests and also in preparation for the IHO elections, I co-authored with an Indian Admiral D.C.Kapoor, a slim book *Maritime Boundary Delimitation*.[13] With the Third Law of the Sea Conference finally adopted in 1982 there was a need for considerable interpretation and this little book fulfilled this.

---

[13] A Kerr and Admiral DC Kapoor, *Maritime Boundary Delimitation*, Carswell, Toronto, 1986

My candidature was successful and I was elected a Director of the IHB in 1987. My co-directors were the UK and Italian candidates, Rear Admiral Sir David Haslam and Rear Admiral Alfredo Civetta. It turned out to be a compatible and successful team. David Haslam had been the Hydrographer of the United Kingdom and had vast administrative experience. As a young Lieutenant Commander, as related earlier, he gave me my first course in hydrography. Alfredo Civetta came from a smaller Hydrographic Office but was most charming and had the useful attribute of speaking both French and English, in addition to his native tongue. The new committee moved into office in September 1987. The routine was for the Conference to first elect the three members of the Directing Committee and then hold a second election to decide which of the three Directors was to be the President. There was no serious contest in this and David Haslam became the President. It is important that the Directing Committee is harmonious because officially each of the three members of the Directing Committee should to have an equal vote on all decisions. The President has a casting vote but ideally it is seldom needed. David Haslam was content to look after administrative matters, including finances, while Alfredo and I looked after the numerous technical matters that had to be decided.

The President was the figurehead of the organisation and by virtue of his position he was provided with a flat in the centre of Monaco. David was a bachelor and this arrangement suited him. Alfredo and I had to provide our own accommodation. I had been advised that we should not live in Monaco as it was expensive and contrary to the situation of many residents there was no tax advantage for the Bureau staff, whose salaries were already tax exempt. Judith and I chose to live in a pretty little French town called Beaulieu sur Mer and my commuting was along the scenic Lower Corniche. When I first took up my post the office was located in a lovely old building beneath the famous Casino but in my second term a new office was built across the harbour that provided more space and convenience. Both of these locations happened to be right beside the track of the Grand Prix and a particular benefit of working in the IHB was to be able to watch, once a year, this famous race just outside my office window.

On arriving in Monaco we felt intimidated by the apparent wealth all around. However, after some time it became clear that although there were many extremely wealthy people there were also many others who worked as accountants and lawyers for the shipping offices, who had no more income than I and like our family, they shopped in the less expensive stores in Nice. A pleasant social mixing point of some of these people was the Monte Carlo Club. This group of English speaking men met once a month for a magnificent lunch at the Hermitage, one of the best hotels in the Principality. Naturally it was washed down with the finest wines and on occasions presided over by the Prince. Particular friends that I met through the Monte Carlo Club were Clive Tinker and his Dutch wife Lisbeth. The Directors were occasionally invited to some of the grand affairs of the

Principality including the Mayor's Candlelight Ball. On this occasion Judith found herself sitting on the left hand of Prince Rainier, who to her delight spoke excellent English and had been at Stowe public school, which he claimed to have much disliked. Princess Grace had been killed in a road accident only a short while before and though people asked Judith to dance with him he politely refused. The Prince's birthday, in November, was a time of great festivities. It started with a reception at the palace at which the scowling princesses were expected to shake hands with the important

Figure 35 The First Directing Committee: RAdm Alfredo Civetta, RAdm David Haslam, Adam J Kerr and Mrs Judith Kerr.

citizens including the three members of the Directing Committee. As at all the grand receptions the choice of drinks was champagne, whisky or orange juice. The following morning there was a Grand Mass in the Cathedral at which all the diplomats dressed in their gold decorated finery and my co-Directors were expected to wear their full ceremonial uniforms of their Admiral's ranks, including their clanking swords. As the only civilian, I had to settle for a morning suit.

After the service the ambassadors would be invited for lunch at the Palace while the rest of us attended a ceremony of awarding the firemen and the police with long service medals. There was much parading of shiny new fire engines and glittering police cars. In the afternoon there was a football game in the Monaco Stadium at which the Directing Committee and their ladies were given the best seats. Prince Rainier was a keen football fan so woe betides the team that might beat Monaco on that day. The final event celebrating the Prince's birthday was a wonderful combined opera and ballet performance in the Salon Garnier. This beautiful ornate theatre is located within the Casino and its design is based on that of the Paris Opera. Various Monagesque dignitaries, including the Prince and the Archbishop, had boxes. On occasions, when not in use by their proper owners, the members of the Directing Committee were given tickets to these boxes.. However during his birthday celebrations the Prince and his family occupied his box and when they arrived, the stirring tune of the Monagesque national anthem struck up and we all stood to attention..

Returning to the work at the IHB the members of the Directing Committee divided the various tasks. A layer of Professional Assistants reported to us and provided us with technical advice. The overall aims of the IHO were to establish standards for the work carried out by the national hydrographic offices, to transfer technology from the developed offices to those less developed and to coordinate new developments that were taking place globally. The organisation produced a number of publications which supported its work these were mainly hard copy but in later years were prepared in digital form. I was assigned to manage the International Hydrographic Review, which contained articles on all new developments and an International Hydrographic Bulletin,

Figure 36 Directing Committee members: Rear Admiral Giuseppe Angisano (Italy), Rear Admiral Chris Andreason (USA) and Adam Kerr (Canada).

which provided more current news. There was an English and a French editor to support this work. The I H Review has been published almost continually since the organisation was formed and provides a long term record extending over eighty years of hydrography's progress and achievements.

An ongoing struggle over the years of the organisation's existence has been whether it was established to support navigation or the wider field of marine science. A particular programme that had been passed to the IHO by Prince Albert I was the General Bathymetric Chart of the Oceans (GEBCO). In the beginning of the twentieth century when the GEBCO programme had started the depths of the World's oceans were a mystery and the thrust of GEBCO was to compile all the scattered and limited number of soundings that were available. In the years after the programme was taken over by the IHO and also by the Intergovernmental Oceanographic Commission (IOC) of UNESCO, there was an accelerating increase in the amount of information available as a result of changing technology. In the nineteen twenties the introduction of acoustic technology resulted in the availability of echo sounders that could provide continuous depth profiles, even in the deepest oceans. Much later, towards the end of the twentieth century, the multibeam echo sounder was developed. This provided a wide swath of depths and eventually led to areas of the seafloor being completely mapped. All this resulted in a great improvement in the GEBCO.[14] A recent step has been to produce this vast amount of data in digital form.

Much of the other work of the IHB concerned the development of standards for navigational information which included standards for both traditional paper charts and for the newly developed digital charts. It was a goal to provide standards for paper charts so that a navigator using charts produced in different countries would see more or less the same things and have the same information with which to navigate. A particular battle over the years was to require all charts to show units of measure, particularly the depth measurements in metric units. Other more subtle things included standardisation of the datums on which hydrographic data was measured. This had become particularly important with the development of the satellite Global Positioning System(GPS) as it is essential that the position of the ship measured by the GPS can be precisely referenced to the position shown on the charts. During my years at the IHB there was a rapid development of electronic or digital charts and the IHO was concerned that these were standardised and safe for navigation.

The Directing Committee, in addition to sharing out the technical work rather grandly split the World into three parts and each Director was responsible for activities in their designated sector. They would then spend time meeting the personnel from the Hydrographic Offices in

---

[14] Jacqueline Campine-Lancre et al, *The History of GEBCO 1903-2003*, GITCbv, Netherlands, 2003.

their sector. I was designated East Asia and Australasia and consequently over the years I developed friendships and close relationships with hydrographers throughout those parts of the World. I was on a first name basis with many hydrographers across the World. The Icelandic Hydrographer, who was also Head of that country's Coast Guard, Hafstein Hafsteinsson became a particular friend.

A difficult problem that we had to deal with was related to the official names to be given to bodies of water. Under a programme started many years before it was decided to develop a publication *Limits of Oceans and Seas* that would provide standard lists of the names so that charts and publications produced by different countries would all call the same body of water by the same name. For most of the World this was not a difficulty but since the Law of the Sea Conferences in the 1950s and 1980s the ocean had become very politicised and names could be construed as a symbol of ownership. Acceptance of the names of bodies of water such as the sea between England and France had long since been reconciled by agreeing to disagree. Today England calls the water between the UK and France the English Channel and France refers to it as Le Manche. Unfortunately Japan and the Koreas had not been so accommodating. Japan insisted on the body of water between Japan and the Korean peninsular being called the Japan Sea, while the Koreans, particularly South Korea, insists that the sea be called the East Sea. Both countries cited historical reasons for their choice. During my time at the IHB and later as a consultant I was invited to several conferences in Seoul, Washington and even Vladivostok to give the IHO's view on the matter which was that it was a technical rather than a political problem. However, to date the countries involved in this particular body of water have been intractable in agreeing to a common name. To Japan it remains the Japan Sea and to the Koreans it remains the East Sea. I continued to be involved in my old interest of the Law of the Sea and the technical matters of Maritime Boundary Delimitation.

I was responsible for editing a *Manual on Technical Aspects of the United Nations Convention on the Law of the Sea – 1982.* In retrospect I have always been rather proud of the fact that a geologist, Dr Mike Keen and I wrote and published in the International Hydrographic Review, a paper that predicted the extreme difficulties that would occur in

Figure 37 Adam Kerr, Johnny Clark, unknown and Prince Rainier III during Conference.

legally interpreting Article 76 on the Definition of the Continental Shelf. This article is highly technical and is used to define areas of the oceans over which States may claim the resources and the area which is, in the words of Ambassador Pardon of Malta 'the common heritage of all mankind.'

Figure 38 Adam Kerr, Prince Albert, Giuseppe Angrisano, and Hans Rohde during Conference.

The IHO's constitution is unusual and pre-dates many of the UN Agencies. The organisation was initially formed in 1921 and its legal mandate took into consideration its world wide scope and the difficulty and cost of holding meetings. Its Directing Committee of three persons is unusual as most UN organisations have a Secretary General, who is advised by a Council or General Assembly . The fact that the IHO only meets every five years in formal conferences is out of date today. In the nineteen twenties persons attending conferences travelled by ship and consequently frequent conference would have been difficult and expensive. Today everyone travels by air, business develops more rapidly and more frequent gatherings are needed. Modern technology and communication can overcome some of the difficulties but there remains the need for an improved system of face to face meetings. However, much of the way business is conducted today in the IHO is governed by an intergovernmental convention and this has proven extremely difficult to change. The Member States of the organisation realise that a different system of management that would permit more frequent meetings, at which key decisions could be made would be an improvement. Unfortunately to change the Convention requires a majority of the Member States' Governments to agree and in many countries this actually requires an agreement of their parliaments. So far this majority has not been achieved and the work of the IHO remains governed by a rather out of date constitution.

The term of election of the Directors is five years but provided they are within the age limit of 65 it is possible to be re-elected for a second term. In 1992 my first term came to an end. David Haslam and Alfredo Civetta had to retire on account of the age limit but Canada agreed to put me up as a candidate for a second term. Once again there was a major conference and an election held. As a returning candidate I was easily elected as a Director for a second term. Elected on that occasion as my co-Directors were an American, Rear Admiral Chris Andreasen and another Italian, Rear Admiral Giuseppe Angrisano. It was felt likely that I, as a returning Director, would then be elected as President. It therefore came as a great shock to find that Admiral Andreasen won by one vote. This was a great disappointment to me but eventually I was able to accept this situation, particularly as Chris Andreasen was a friendly and understanding compatriot. Once again the duties were divided and the Directing Committee got into its new term. During my second term I found that the work on developing standards for the digital charts had greatly increased. Much of the work was to develop very complex standards for the construction and navigational use of the Electronic Chart Display and Information System[15] and also for the formats to be used for the exchange of the digital data, which was rapidly replacing the hard copy paper charts. There was considerable interaction with the United Nation's International Maritime Organisation (IMO) and I found myself frequently at meetings at its Headquarters in London. The United Kingdom Hydrographic Office was much involved in the new technology and was represented in several of the working groups related to the standards. I was consequently in close contact with the UK Hydrographer and many of his professional staff.

Domestic arrangements had settled down. Initially we had moved through several different houses in Beaulieu sur

---

[15] Horst Hecht (Ed) *The Electronic Chart*, Geomares 2011. Third Edition.

Mer and nearby Eze. One house was on the Moyenne Corniche near the historic village of Eze. It had spectacular views but Judith thought that it was haunted! It was rented from an English woman who at the time was driving a taxi in Monaco. Apparently she had been married to an Italian and a great mystery was that his considerable amount of climbing gear remained in the cellar of the house. Was he pushed or did he fall! We never found out. One day Judith suggested that as we were paying such vast sums in rent that we should buy a boat and live aboard it. 'My Dear.' I said. 'I have wanted to do that all my life!' The result was a search of the nearby ports for a suitable boat and we found a 45 foot American Petersen sloop called *Chesapeake.*

Compared with many other boats on that coast it was not big but provided good space for Judith and I and the two young boys. Initially we lived on the boat at Antibes, where we had a berth but later moved closer to Monaco. However getting a permanent home for the boat was difficult and expensive. For most of one winter we lived on it at Beaulieu and later found a berth in Fontvielle, the back port of Monaco We lived aboard *Chesapeake* for a year but kept a small flat ashore to store our belongings. The weather was warm enough and the boat well fitted out for living aboard but the long hours of darkness during the winter proved trying. During the summers we invited friends and sailed the 100 miles over to Corsica and south to Sardinia. The coast along the South of France is not ideal for cruising as there are only limited areas of refuge but trips were made to such exotic places as St Tropez and Port Grimaud.

Figure 39 45-foot American sloop *Chesapeake*.

The summer trips to Corsica and Sardinia were memorable. It is about 100 nautical miles across from the mainland at Monaco to the closest point of Corsica, usually Calvi. With luck that trip can be done in about twenty four hours but the Mediterranean can be fickle and while it can be a calm crossing there is always the possibility of encountering the fierce mistral. This wind comes out of the Gulf of Lyons but due to the intense heating of the high island of Corsica the wind strength is increased as it approaches the West coast of that island. There are several beautiful sandy havens along that coast but one must take care to avoid the mistral. Another difficulty of sailing in those islands during the high summer season is the huge invasion of Italian boats. Coming into the marinas in the evening there was always a struggle to find a berth and particularly to obtain power and water from the service posts along the dock. As there seemed to be little standardisation of the electric terminals there was frequently much fumbling trying to connect the correct plug. All this while the posts also provided the source of water. It is a wonder that no one was electrocuted.

We experienced another man made hazard one year when we decided to sail from the Straits of Bonafacio to Elba. We were sailing happily along with the boys catching the occasional bonito – yes, they do exist in the Mediterranean - when our course took us close to the island of Pianosa. The chart told us that this was a prison island and as we got closer we were looking at the guard towers. Suddenly from the back of the island came a small grey ship roaring towards us. As it got closer their uniformed crew shouted at us to stop. However, as we had a large spinnaker set this proved to be a slower operation that the Italian crew would like and they became excited and agitated.. Eventually we were able to slow down sufficiently for them to come alongside. They were not happy by our proximity to the island and demanded all our passports. Presumably the suspicion was that we were from the Mafia trying to arrange an escape. While their colleagues investigated our passports with numerous radio calls, our more attractive ladies were busy chatting up the young Italian crew. After a lengthy time they must have decided that we were no threat and we were told to get on our way and sail away from the island

Another saga of our ownership of *Chesapeake* occurred not long after we had bought the boat. During the Monaco Grand Prix many beautiful yachts come into the port and someone suggested to me that we should ask the harbourmaster, with whom the IH Bureau was on good terms, if it was possible to have a berth for my boat during the event. I thought it would be a better if one of our French speaking staff made the approach. He came back after visiting the harbourmaster to say that he had not thought it a good idea as *Chesapeake,* being a relatively small sailing yacht, would not provide a good platform for viewing the race as it would be too low. Most of the yachts were large motor yachts with a high vantage point on their bridges. How naive I was because the next day the Times published an article discussing the huge fees, amounting to £ 10,000s that were being paid to secure a berth! As it was the IH

Bureau already had a prime place for watching the race with the office right beside the track. In fact one of the benefits was that while we could sip our champagne from crystal flutes and observe the race from our office window, the unfortunate public had either to rent spaces in the adjacent buildings at huge cost or sit in the stands, exposed to the elements and drink out of plastic bottles and cups because plastic was not permitted near the track!

Commuting to work from a boat presented a few problems but it provided a venue for entertaining our friends. The boys had moved from the local French school at Beaulieu to a large school near the Palace, on the Rock at Monaco This was not officially an international school but had a high percentage of students from international countries. We had decided from the start that the boys would be totally immersed in French speaking schools and this paid dividends in the years ahead, although it was no doubt difficult for them initially. An early decision that we had made on arriving at Monaco was to replace our old Golden Retriever 'Captain.' Before leaving Canada we had decided that a large dog would not fit in well with our life style in Monaco and the French Riviera and we left 'Captain' in the hands of our neighbours who had two sons close in age to ours. My family for many years kept Dandie Dinmont Terriers and in fact the Bergs, my previous wife Liv and I had brought the breed from England and Linda Bergh had championed her dogs through both the Canadian and American show rings. We could not locate a Dandie Dinmont and decided to move to a quite similar breed, at least in appearance. This was the Wire Haired Dachshund . We arranged for a friend in the UK to find us a puppy. Our little puppy arriving at Nice airport was the pepper and salt colouring and was called Piglet. Before long everyone loved this little dog and she went everywhere with us, even on our long sailing trips to Corsica and Sardinia.

In the ten years at the IHB in Monaco from 1987 to 1997, the work was demanding, as was the social life. Judith, who had given up full time work as a nurse joined the 'Odd Group,' a group of primarily amateur artists. This group met once a week under the guidance of a most charming man, John Pelling, who had been both a priest and an artist. A high point during the year was for the 'Odd Group' to spend a long weekend in western Provence. As it was May the weather was usually most pleasant and husbands were invited. Fine meals were enjoyed and days out sketching usually included sipping Pernod. John Pelling liked to celebrate the death of Aubrey Beardsley, whose tomb is located in the grave yard above Menton, and members of the group also took part. These gatherings brought together an eclectic group of ex-patriots. Aubrey Beardsley, known for his erotic drawings, had contacted tuberculosis in the years after the First World War and had moved to Menton, where he died. Another social gathering in Monaco was the weekly meetings of a Scottish country dance group. The group was led by Jennifer Fletcher and was taken up enthusiastically by the expatriate community. It is said that your ability (or inability) to perform in Scottish Country dancing is related to your IQ and I did not want to verify that matter. Once a year there was a ball and over the years the men, including me, acquired kilts. A memorable trip arranged for the British community by Michael Healey, a retired British naval officer, was to go aboard a British warship during the French fleet review that was set to commemorate the landings on the South coast of France during World War ll. A flotilla of over 50 warships snaked along the coast from Monaco to Toulon with two French aircraft carriers providing the viewing stand for the dignitaries. During the afternoon small boats, often with beautiful French ladies aboard tantalised the sailors on the warships, who were expected to line the rails in their spotless white uniforms as the scantily clad young ladies cruised below in their yachts..

In 1997 the pleasant years in Monaco came to an end and we made plans for a second retirement. Our older son Andrew had been sent off to a public school at Kelly College in Devon, while Tim our younger son stayed on in the French system to the end. One matter to consider was what to do with *Chesapeake*. For several years it had been used mainly for recreation along the French coast and across to Corsica. One year the family had sailed it to the Ballearic Islands. Towards the end of our stay it had been possible to rent a convenient berth in Fontvielle, which is the reclaimed harbour on the western side of Monaco This was convenient as it was possible to walk to and from the office. It was particularly good as a place to stay as we could easily walk home. At that time the Prince had a zoo built on the side of the rock on which the palace was situated. Exotic animals that had been given to the Prince at various times were in cages. At night we could lie in our bunks on *Chesapeake* and hear the lions roaring or the monkeys chattering. Later, people who felt this enclosure was unkind to the animals argued that it should be closed down. The Prince kept another collection of animals at his farm on Mont Agel, a mountain that dominated the coast above Monaco We often walked in that area and you could look down on the large animals that the Prince kept there. During the summer of 1996 we made plans sail *Chesapeake* to England in preparation for our move there. Although it is possible to take a boat of *Chesapeake's* size up the Rhone River and into the French canal system, coming out at Rouen, it was decided that this was lengthy and hard. An alternative is to pass through the Canal du Midi into the Bay of Biscay but the depths were marginal to allow passage for this boat. In the end it was decided to pass through the Straits of Gibraltar and across the Bay of Biscay. As most of my crew had limited free time a group of Norwegian friends took the boat to Almunecar on the south coast of Spain. We joined the boat there. My son Andrew and various friends, including Michel Huet, who had worked with me at Monaco, made up the crew. The trip through the Straits of Gibraltar was rough with strong head winds prevailing up the Portuguese coast. Never-the-less in spite of these adverse conditions plus a malfunctioning engine *Chesapeake* entered Lorient, where Judith and our son Tim joined for the final leg to Cornwall.

In May 1997 a new team of directors was elected and in August I left the IHB and went to live at Flagstaff Cottage, the old family home in Cornwall. A discussion had taken place on where the family should live at the end of my second retirement, and it was decided to move to Cornwall rather than Canada. My mother had died several years before and I had inherited the old family home at Lamorna.

A final note on my ten years at the IHB was that I was awarded a Monagesque medal, the Croix de St George for my work at the IHB. While this was gratifying the shine was partly taken from it when the same medal was awarded the next year to the Spanish Professional Assistant, who I felt had made very limited contribution to the organisation and in fact seemed to have actually worked against it by stirring up the staff on various domestic issues.

RE-ESTABLISHING IN LAMORNA

Figure 40 Carn Dhu, the view from Flagstaff Cottage in Winter.

During the years since my Mother had died in 1990, Judith and I had let out Flagstaff Cottage, using it ourselves during the summer. Before settling there to live some major refurbishments were made and my grandfather's studio, beside the stream, had been converted from a day studio to a residence. Initially it had been rented to young artists but much later it was further improved and let through an agency. Returning to my roots in Lamorna was a wonderful experience. There were still many people I knew. I had thought at first that my long cherished dream of becoming an artist would finally come true. During my many years in Canada I had often considered returning to Lamorna to work as an artist on the one hand and fish commercially on the other. During my teens before I went to Canada I had worked for a while commercially fishing for mackerel, more as a pastime than a serious money making venture. When we did finally get back to Lamorna in 1997 it was Judith who took up painting seriously and enrolled for a BA in Fine Art at Falmouth School of Art.

Before I had actually retired from Monaco, Barbara Bond, the Deputy Director of the UK Hydrographic Office at Taunton, had asked me if I was interested in being a consultant on electronic chart production. That was directly in line with my interests and I agreed. It was in fact ironic that I should find myself working for the UK Hydrographic Office because for many years I had been very critical of that organisation. The Hydrographic Office has an excellent world wide reputation but in my years in Canada I had decided that it was overbearingly arrogant with an attitude that anything produced in its ex-colonies was inferior to that made in the United Kingdom. In Canada it was felt that the United Kingdom Hydrographic Office stressed too much its past glory established by Captain Cook and others, while in Canada we were forward looking and much more progressive and innovative. There was no question that the UKHO was most meticulous in both its surveys and chart production but it was very slow to develop and accept new digital technology that I was keen to see developed. Still I was determined to provide some consultancy to that organisation and to encourage the adoption of the technology. I was given very direct access to the Chief

Hydrographer, Rear Admiral Johnny Clark, which was helpful. The British Government, under Margaret Thatcher, had unfortunately developed the idea of Trading Funds in which an organisation such as the Hydrographic Office was expected to pay its own way. This might have been a good thing except it put it in strong competition with commercial firms that were also producing navigational charts. I was of the opinion that some of the most innovative work was being done by the commercial companies such as C-Map and Navionics but the UKHO tended to criticise these companies on the grounds that their products were unreliable. I continued to work for the UKHO for several years and enjoyed my contacts with the Hydrographers and their staff but realised that my main value was in my external contacts and these were gradually disappearing. In mutual agreement with the Chief Hydrographer Dr Wyn Williams, I decided in 2000 to cease the consultancy.

I next formed an alliance with several of my old colleagues from the Canadian Hydrographic Service, Steve MacPhee and Ross Douglas, with a retired Chief Dutch Hydrographer, Rear Admiral Hans van Opstal and a retired South African Hydrographer, Rear Admiral Neil Guy. We formed International Hydrographic Management Consulting.(IHMC) We were all extremely experienced hydrographers. We possibly had short comings in the details of the modern technology but were well placed to assist hydrographic organisations around the World in setting up and managing their affairs. During its existence IHMC was involved in several international projects. One of these was to advise the UK Maritime Coastguard Agency (MCA) in setting up its hydrographic survey programme. It was not commonly known that MCA had this responsibility because most of the work had been done under contract both to commercial firms and to the naval survey service itself. IHMC came to the conclusion that commercial contracts were more cost effective than those carried out by the Navy. It also felt that more use should be made of new technology, such as the use of airborne laser technology and the new multi-beam acoustic technology. There is no doubt that our advice and recommendations appeared to criticise the approach that had been taken by the UKHO and the Naval Survey Service and won us some enemies.

In a second contract IHMC advised the Coast Guard Agency on how to maintain the charts around the British Isles. For certain areas, notably the Thames Estuary and the Straits of Dover, the sea floor sediments are extremely mobile and consequently the topography of the sea floor is constantly changing. As ship owners were expecting their ships to go into ports with less and less clearance between their keels and the sea bottom to maximise the amount of cargoes carried. It was vitally important that these changes be regularly and precisely monitored, especially relevant in the approaches to the Thames and in the English Channel, where ships with draughts of over 20 metres had to pass through waters that were in places only a few metres deeper than the keels of the ships. IHMC presented various suggestions on the technology and establishing the optimum interval of monitoring in order to minimise the costs of dredging and ensure the safety of the very large ships which are today passing through British waters. Another consultancy was to assist the Hydrographic Office of Mozambique in setting up its work. Although Norway and the UK had already given the country considerable assistance it was short of both equipment and technical knowledge. In such developing countries it is always difficult to maintain the high technical standards necessary to ensure reliable charts and navigation.

Apart from IHMC I was referred by the President of the IHO to the International Court of Justice (ICJ) in the Hague to provide some cartographic advice on two different bilateral maritime boundary disputes that the Court had been asked to arbitrate. The first of these was the boundary in the Caribbean between Nicaragua and Honduras, The second was in the Black Sea and the boundary between the Ukraine and Romania. The International Court of Justice is established in the magnificent Peace Palace in the Hague and the learned Judges have the most excellent offices and supporting staff. A team of lawyers helps them research their decisions. I worked directly with the lawyers but from time to time would be summoned by individual judges to advise on various geographic matters. My advice was mainly on the geographic situation in connection with the disputed boundaries and some cartographic representations of the various options. Both the judgements were much influenced by the presence of offshore islands. In the Caribbean there were numerous small islets called Cays of which some were inhabited and some not. Islands are a special topic treated by the UN Law of the Sea Treaty in Article 121 and these were a particular case because both their geographic position and their sovereignty lacked precision. After we had studied the geographical situation in depth and the judgement had been made a hurricane swept through the area destroying several of these important reference points. In the Black Sea a large remote island called Serpent Island became a key geographic feature to be considered. Its status as being able to support human habitation, a test for its relevance in establishing its jurisdiction, was an important part of Ukraine's case. In the end a compromise was made that partially supported both claims. My background at the University of Wales and my earlier studies on the regime of islands were most helpful in providing cartographic advice on these two disputes

For another consultancy for the World Bank, administered through the South African Maritime organisation, IHMC was re-established. This work was in connection with a major project, termed the Marine Electronic Highway that was to improve the navigation of the numerous large ships, mostly oil tankers, that travelled from the Persian Gulf, through the Mozambique Channel and around South Africa. IHMC's part in this multi-million dollar study that involved visits to Kenya, Tanzania, the Seychelles, Mauritius and Mozambique, was quite small. The task was to visit the maritime authorities in these countries in the West Indian Ocean to examine their capabilities in providing services, in the way of charts and other navigational aids. Unfortunately the development of the Electronic Highway coincided with the surge in piracy based in Somalia that was taking place and ships were forced far out in the Indian Ocean rather than through the Mozambique Channel. My Dutch colleague, Rear Admiral van Opstal, and I provided the hydrographic part of the team and a South African provided the expertise on navigational aids and services. A side benefit of this trip was to be driven by our South African colleague from Pretoria to Maputo in Mozambique. On the return trip a detour was made through the Kruger National Park, a wonderful place.

Throughout my work with IHMC and my own consultancy to the ICJ I had continued to edit the International Hydrographic Review (IHR). As a Director at the IHB I had supervised the production of the IHR and the IH Bulletin but

Figure 41 Rear Admiral Steve Ritchie and Prince Rainer lll.

shortly after I left that office a decision was made to stop the publication. This was met with some resistance by hydrographic practitioners and it was decided that a Dutch publishing company should be given the rights to produce the journal under the copyright of the IHO. I was contracted by the Dutch company GITC and asked to be the editor.

Editing a semi-scientific journal is demanding. On the one hand there is the continual search for copy and as hydrographers are not bound by any 'publish or perish' policy of truly academic publications it is difficult for them to give up their already heavy workload to write learned articles. Never-the-less I set up a system of peer review which ensured that most of the papers published were of acceptable quality. Although editing the IHR was hard work it kept me in continuous touch with the hydrographic community and in particular with some of the up and coming young scientists. Jack Wallace of the Hydrographic Society of America was particularly supportive of my editorial work and funded my travel to several conferences to meet prospective authors.

There came a time when the commercial production of the Review was no longer covering its costs and it was decided that the IHB should once again resume its production but only in digital form. Dave Wells and other academics strongly supported the continuance of the publication. I was asked if I would continue as editor for two more years and at the end of that time the task was passed on to Ian Halls in New Zealand. Throughout my several careers I have written over 50 papers on hydrography, marine cartography and subjects related to it, such as the Law of the Sea. I was asked to contribute four short papers dealing with marine cartography to a very major publication on the History of Cartography. This important scientific work is now in the final stages of publication by the University of Chicago Press.[16]

Before leaving my hydrographic career I would be remiss not to mention my long and close friendship with Rear Admiral Steve Ritchie. This wonderful man died only a few years ago in his nineties. He had been a hydrographic surveyor in the UK Hydrographic Service for many years and had ended up as the UK Hydrographer. He told many interesting stories of his surveys in remote parts of the World, particularly in the Pacific Ocean. Some of his books are quite biographical[17] and relate many of the interesting phases of his life. To me he served as a great role model. He was flamboyant in his appearance and dress and in his older years his ruddy face and curly white hair along with his choice of bright clothes, particularly his red socks, stood him out from the crowd. He preceded David Haslam as both the UK Hydrographer and as the president of the IHO. During the latter posting, which he held for ten years, he managed to oversee the drafting of that organisation's convention. He loved to have a good time and when he was in command of HMS *Dalrymple* he became involved with the Mardi Gras bands in Trinidad and dressed up as a butterfly he joined a

[16] See Appendix.

[17] See *No Day Too Long – An Hydrographer's Tale*, Pentland Press, 1991 and *The Life of the Survey Ship Challenger*, Hollis & Carter, 1957.

band and participated in the festival. On an occasion of a party arranged by the Hydrographic Society, of which he was the president, in the run up to Christmas one year, this ruddy and slightly rotund admiral could be seen dressed in a Santa Claus costume dancing happily with a beautiful American girl. In his retirement he went to live on the Scottish coast, north of Aberdeen and we would often compare the weather and sea conditions between his remote location at Ellon and my own situation in Lamorna.

A FINAL CAREER – THE CORNISH MARITIME TRUST

My career as a hydrographic consultant and editor was beginning to wind down and in 2005 I was invited to join the Cornish Maritime Trust (CMT) as a trustee and since then this has provided me with an active final career. The CMT was formed in 1990 and its prime objective was to maintain the Cornish heritage in historic working boats. In particular it was directed at providing examples of the different rigs used. Although several larger traditional boats once graced the seas around the West Country, such as the Falmouth Packets and the Brixham trawlers, the huge fleets of luggers that once dominated every West Country port, figure large in the maritime history of the region. Oyster dredgers are also historically important and even today it is only permitted to dredge for oysters on the Truro River and the Helford River under sail. So the particular craft used for this occupation are also part of a heritage that should be maintained. In 2005, when I joined the Trust its oldest and most well known craft, the lugger *Barnabas* that had been originally built at St Ives in 1881, was in a poor state and was considered unseaworthy. My task was to raise the funds needed for a complete renovation. Fortunately the Heritage Lottery Fund offered a possible source for these funds. The requirement was that the Trust had to find 25% of the funds needed but some of this could be in kind. If the application was successful the remainder of the funding would come from the Lottery fund. I was not unfamiliar with the process of acquiring grants from similar work in Canada and approval was given for the funding. Several boat builders in the West Country were asked to bid on the work and the contract was given to R Cann Ltd, a company based in Totnes but it was required that the work be carried out, under a sub-contractual arrangement, in Penzance. Maintaining a heritage boat is fraught with difficulty as critics are always ready to say that the repaired boat is not the original. On the other hand it is not possible to carry out a re-novation that lea-ves rot and other weaknesses in the boat.

Figure 42 SS 634 *Barnabas* at Sea (Courtesy Cornish Maritime Trust).

The renovation of *Barnabas* was completed in 2006 but that was not to be the end. The shipwright who had done the work was undoubtedly highly skilled and had done a good job but he had turned out to be a very poor money manager. Several months after the work had been accepted the CMT were approached by lawyers for the shipwright arguing that the Trust owed the contractor £ 60,000 in 'extras!' This came as an unexpected shock and even more so when a writ was placed on the boat. There followed the best part of a year of legal arguing in which the only winners seemed to be the lawyers and the matter was finally settled out of court costing the CMT an amount it could ill afford. In the years since the Trust has rallied and has carried out an active programme. The CMT also owns the oyster dredger *Soft Wing* which had enjoyed an earlier renovation courtesy of the Heritage Lottery Fund. This boat is active, sailing mostly in Falmouth waters. Another much smaller open boat *Ellen*, had originally been of a class known as Gorran Haven Crabbers. These boats were cleverly designed with a sprit rig that allowed a single fisherman to work the boat on the inshore crab fishery in the area of Mevagissey. My task in all this was to help manage the boats, including their maintenance and to organise the summer sailing programme. It had been decided by the Trust to code the two larger vessels under the Coastguard regulations and to require the skippers to have some minimum qualification. In the case of *Barnabas* this was a Yacht master's certificate with commercial endorsements. My own certificate as a foreign going master mariner had long since become obsolete and so I returned to school once more to study for and obtain a yacht master's certificate. In 2012 the Trust was asked to participate in the Queen's Jubilee Pageant on the River Thames and I arranged and participated on this great trip of *Barnabas*, sailing it from Cornwall and back and participating in the Pageant.

The trip to and from the Thames from Cornwall was an excitement itself. We enjoyed fair winds up the Channel and went first into Faversham on the north Kent coast. This was a different kind of sailing from the West Coiuntry. A narrow, shallow and winding river led from the Thames Estuary several miles inland. The trip had to be undertaken at extreme high tide. On the way we passed several large Thames Sailing barges, and wondered how these huge craft were able to navigate the narrow and shallow river. On reaching Faversham we went alongside the Iron Quay, where there was a charming traditional boat yard run by a friend Alan Reekie. As the tide dropped we settled on the soft mud. The weather was unusually warm and beautiful and we enjoyed several days in Faversham. During this time we lowered the foremast and replaced the mizzen mast by a special stub mast that we had had made. The overall objective was to lower the height from the waterline to the top of our rigging to 5 metres so that when we went up and down the Thames we could pass under the low bridges. We moved from Faversham through the Swale and inside the Isle of Sheppey. From there we went up the Thames to the West India Dock, where we had to undergo various briefings and safety inspections. On the day before the Pageant we were required to go up the River to our appointed moorings. This was cleverly arranged so that when we did start we simply had to let go our moorings and we were in exactly the relative position to the nearby boats as we would occupy during the trip down river. On the day of the Pageant itself the weather forecast was poor with heavy rain forecast and that was how it turned out. We started in good conditions but by the time we had reached the City of London it was raining hard. We were most happy to fight our way through the motor yachts and get into the West India lock The homeward trip to Cornwall was not as smooth as our outward trip. After calling in at Faversham to pick up and re-rig our masts we had a spell of persistent westerly winds that delayed our trip home.

Another major venture for this boat during 2015 was to sail Barnabas around Britain to follow the tracks of the Cornish fishing fleets of the nineteenth century that chased the herring. This epic voyage took ten weeks to travel north through the Irish Sea and across Scotland through the Caledonian Canal. It then went north to Wick and from there to the Orkneys and Shetland Islands before returning to Cornwall via the North Sea and English Channel. I took part as skipper on some of the key parts of the trip, in particular the part around northern Scotland., Considering the complex logistics of this trip in which crews, including skippers, had to be changed every week, the overall trip went remarkably well with no one was hurt and no damage occurred to the boat. Unfortunately we experienced a lot of head winds which led to a heavy use of the diesel engine. The Cornish fishing fleets of the nineteenth century are reported to have sailed as far as Balta Sound on the extreme northern end of the Shetland Islands. Sadly the northerly head winds prevented us from making that goal but we did make it to

Lerwick where we were most hospitably received. During the Scottish part of the trip we met similar organisations to our own that were busy maintaining their heritage of boats similar to our own Cornish lugger, in the form of Fyfies and Zulues. Like the Pageant trip we experienced adverse head winds on the way home although this time on the way through the North Sea and rounding the Thames Estuary.

A Continuing Interest in Fine Art

Judith has pursued art professionally since we returned to Cornwall, spending seven years at Falmouth University, School of Art and obtaining a BA. I have been more involved in the administration of art. As the grandson of SJ Lamorna Birch RA, RWS, the distinguished academician, I have been persuaded by various institutions to share what I know about his life, his work and my involvement with them.

I was invited to be the President of the Lamorna Society, a group that had been formed to secure the memory of my grandfather and the group of artists that he had gathered in Lamorna. This group had been formed after the publication of a book "The Painter Laureate" written by Austin Wormleighton, just before I had returned to live in Cornwall again. The group has actively pursued these interests since then and meets annually in Lamorna. It produces an interesting quarterly publication dealing with artistic called *Flagstaff*.

I also accepted an invitation to be a trustee of the Newlyn Passmore Edwards Gallery, and later became secretary to the Board of Trustees. This organisation is a charity that owns and is responsible for the upkeep of the gallery. The ongoing health of this gallery, built in 1896 in Newlyn, is specified in an Indenture drafted when it was built. At that time there was a very thriving group of artists, called the Newlyn School, working in Newlyn and the surrounding district and the gallery was built and made available to foster these practitioners of fine art. While the main responsibility of the Board of Trustees is to maintain the upkeep and general financial well being of the gallery one clause attempts to specify its use. It reads as follows:

> *for use as a Gallery for the exhibition of pictures and other works of art and for the advancement of painting and the other arts and the encouragement of the popular interest in and appreciation of the same and all purposes connected therewith and generally for the use and benefit of the Artists residing at Newlyn or Penzance or in the neighbourhood....*

Unfortunately this clause is subject to very contentious interpretation. This is partly due to the dating of the drafting being over 100 years old and partly to the form of language used. Over the years the gallery has lived through periods of poverty and wealth and at present it enjoys considerable patronage from the Arts Council of England. There is an ongoing debate over the use of the institution and on its availability to show the works of local artists or international art that is fostered by the Arts Council. There is an ongoing debate on whether the art shown should be contemporary work by living artists or work that may be classified of the genre Contemporary, such as installations and abstract work. The previous chairman Jeremy LeGrice, an outgoing and outspoken artist, now unfortunately deceased, whose family had financed the original land on which the gallery was built, tackled the matter head on but the organisation holding the long term lease, Newlyn Gallery Ltd. could not support his views that the gallery should be primarily used to show the work of local artists. As the Secretary I have tried to remain neutral in this debate although personally I would be happier to see the gallery used to show local artists' work to a much greater extent. I have tried hard to understand the move to abstract art and the move away from representational art. In Cornwall it originally found a footing in the group of artists that established themselves in St. Ives under artists such as Ben Nicholson, Christopher Wood, Peter Lanyon and Barbara Hepworth in the 1940s. Even the work of primitives, such as Alfred Wallis leaves me cold.

In maritime painting I favour the beautifully drawn paintings of artists such as Napier Hemy and Henry Scott Tuke This trend away from technically well drafted art is not of course just a Cornish phenomenon but is an international change led by such well acclaimed artists as Picasso, Chagall and many others. Never the less it fails to win my admiration. However I fear I am fighting a losing battle and must reluctantly accept this movement of contemporary art. The Turner Prize says it all. What is art? Living much of my life as a sailor who must deal with precise and accurate information the emotions that drive modern art do not have a place. My taste for art and particularly my personal views on the Newlyn Gallery and the current exhibition programme have put me somewhat at odds with my wife Judith who as a recent graduate of an art school, has much greater sympathy with the development of modern art than I who am rather conservative in my artistic taste.

And now ... I come to the end of my book, the autobiography of Adam Kerr, chartmaker, fisherman and sailor. The book has focussed mainly on my experiences in the Antarctic and Arctic but also recorded my early years in Cornwall and my later years, when I was lucky enough to be elected a member of the Directing Committee of the International Hydrographic Bureau at Monaco.

During my working years I was fortunate enough to meet and work with many interesting people who greatly enhanced my knowledge and experience. In thinking back on my origins I am incredibly grateful to my parents and my maternal grandfather who steered me on to such an interesting life. Their own illustrious lives provided my model.

Art has been all around throughout my life and it has found its way into my own interests. My grandfather, S J Lamorna Birch RA, RWS was a masterful painter. My mother was also an artist and my two sons have artistic ability. Throughout my life I have been torn by my interest as a sailor, both professional and recreational and my interest in the arts and in writing. My father was a writer with over fifty books published. I have put pen to paper in books and technical papers that record some of the matters that concerned me the most (see Appendix).

Time will tell how much I have been able to contribute to the World around me. When I consider the exploits of many in the maritime field of hydrography and marine science in general I doubt that my own record will stand out but hopefully my own contribution will have helped the overall level of knowledge. My career has coincided with an incredible time of technical advance that has paralleled much larger developments in the World in general. Apart from the very specific developments in polar charting I have seen our ability to position ourselves at sea and go from sextant observations to the Global Positioning System (GPS). I have seen the technology take us from depths measured by lead line to multibeam echo sounders. In the processing of data I have watched the technology take us from hand held calculators used to calculate geodetic positions to a totally computer driven system of e-navigation that provides everything from Electronic Chart and Information Systems (ECDIS) to collision avoidance. In the particular field of polar surveying I have participated in developing methods to measure the water depth beneath pack ice of more than two metres thickness. This has been achieved by blasting holes, by drilling and by acoustic means. I have also participated in the development of remote controlled vehicles that can carry out measurements beneath the floating ice surface.

My own participation in some of these developments may have been minor and at times tedious and bureaucratic but I count myself very fortunate that I was there at all. I would never have believed all this when I left my Cornish village of Lamorna sixty years ago.

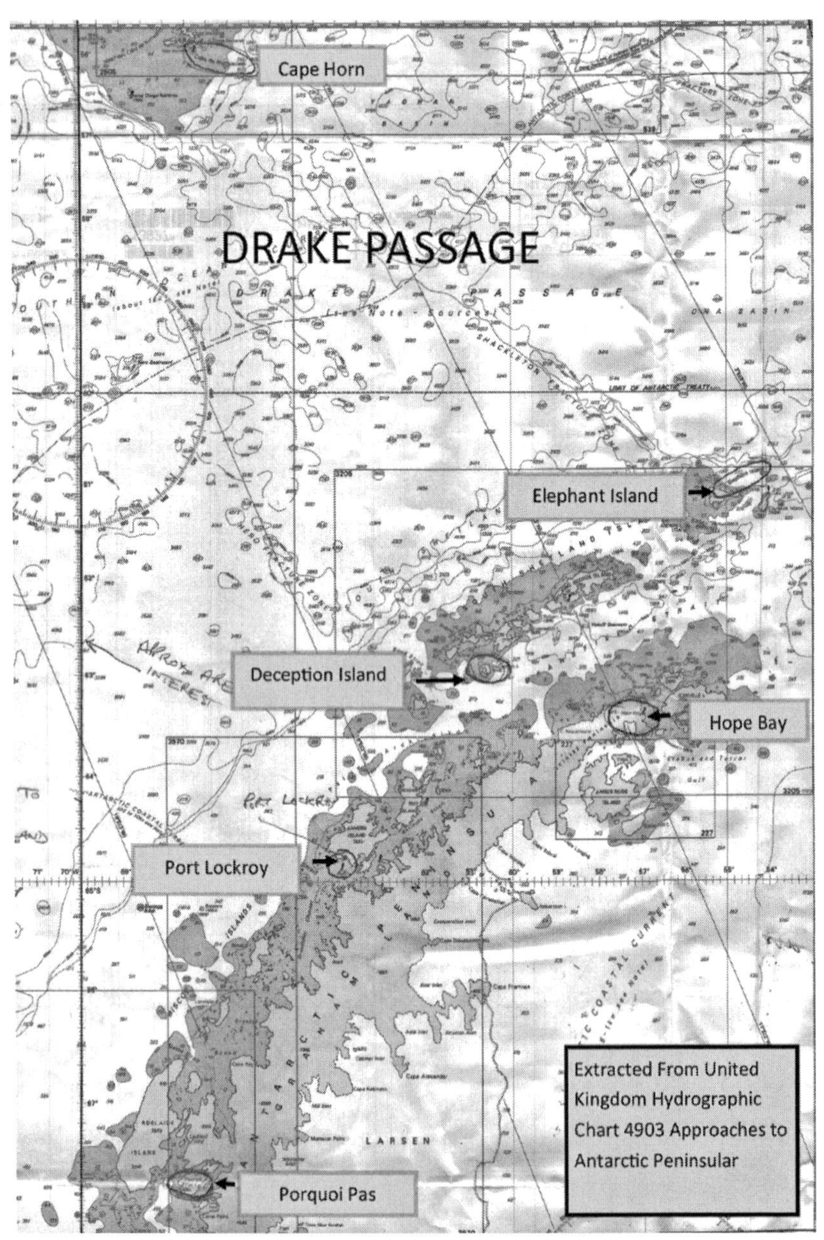
Cape Horn
DRAKE PASSAGE
Elephant Island
Deception Island
Hope Bay
Port Lockroy
Porquoi Pas
Extracted From United Kingdom Hydrographic Chart 4903 Approaches to Antarctic Peninsular

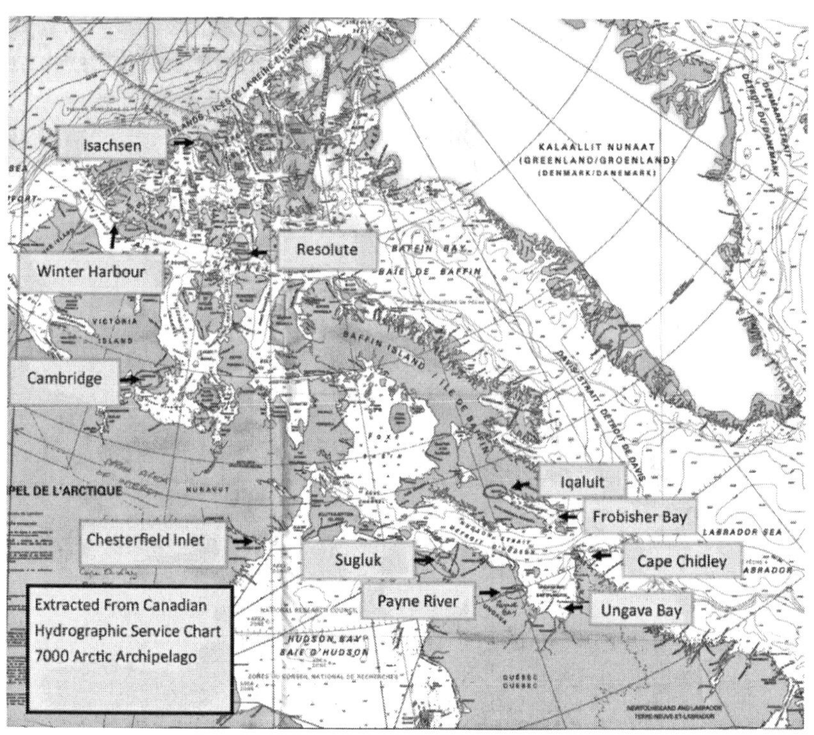
Isachsen
Winter Harbour
Resolute
Cambridge
Iqaluit
Frobisher Bay
Chesterfield Inlet
Sugluk
Cape Chidley
Payne River
Ungava Bay
KALAALLIT NUNAAT
(GREENLAND/GROENLAND)
(DENMARK/DANEMARK)
BAFFIN BAY
BAIE DE BAFFIN
BAFFIN ISLAND / ILE DE BAFFIN
DAVIS STRAIT / DETROIT DE DAVIS
LABRADOR SEA
HUDSON BAY
BAIE D'HUDSON
PEL DE L'ARCTIQUE
VICTORIA ISLAND
Extracted From Canadian
Hydrographic Service Chart
7000 Arctic Archipelago

Select Bibliography of papers and publications that represent my work and my interests.

AJ Kerr 'HYPOS - A system for Processing Hydrographic Survey data', *Int. Hydrographic Review* XLVI (2) July 1969.

AJ Kerr, *Oceanographic Cartography*, Edited collection papers, International Cartographic Association 1972.

AJ Kerr, 'A survey of the plotter routines for survey and chart lattices in the Canadian Hydrographic Service'. *Proceedings of Eleventh Annual Canadian Hydrographic Conference*, Ottawa 1972.

AE Collin, D Monahan and AJ Kerr, 'Navigators aren't the only Sea Chart users', Oceanic papers presented at the *6th Technical Conference of the ICA*, Ottawa. August 1972.

AJ Kerr, 'Arctic Hydrography - A pre-requisite for resource development', presented at twenty eighth meeting of the *Institute of Navigation*, June 29 1972

AJ Kerr, 'Recent changes in Canadian Sailing Directions', *Int. Hydrographic Review* Vol LI (1) January 1974.

AJ Kerr, 'The Multi-faceted Education of the Hydrographer', *Proceedings of the International Federation of Surveyors*, Commission 2, September 1974.

AJ Kerr, 'Chart Design Considerations for the Navigators of Today and Tomorrow', *Int. Hydrographic Review*, Vol LIII, (1) 1976.

AJ Kerr, 'Development of Through - Ice Hydrographic Surveying', *International Federation of Surveyors,* Commission 4, 1977 Stockholm.

AJ Kerr, 'Delimitation of the Continental Shelf between the United Kingdom of Great Britain and the French Republic MSc Thesis, Department of Law, University of Wales,1978.

AJ Kerr, 'Wave Information and the Yachtsman', presented at the *Wave Information Workshop,* Bedford Institute of Oceanography, October 1980.

AJ Kerr, 'The Use of Cartography in the Law of the Sea Negotiations', *10th International Cartographic Conference,* Tokyo, August 1980.

AJ Kerr (Ed), *Dynamics of Oceanic Cartography,* Commission Report to the International Cartographic Conference, September 1980.

AJ Kerr and PK Mukerjee, 'Who is Qualified to Survey Canada's Offshore? *Canadian Institute of Surveying Conference* May 1981.

AJ Kerr and NM Anderson, 'Communication and the Nautical Chart', *Journal of Navigation,* Volume 35, No.3 1982.

AJ Kerr, 'The Training of Hydrographers and Marine Cartographers', *Proceedings of the Conference of Commonwealth Surveyors,* Cambridge, Paper N L4 1983.

NM Anderson and AJ Kerr, 'Exploring Arctic Seas –Today and

Yesterday', *Leadline to Laser, Centennial Conference*, Canadian Hydrographic Service 1983.

AJ Kerr, 'Navigation Chart Design', *Royal Institute Navigation Seminar*, London 1984. Subsequently published in the *Journal of Navigation*.

AJ Kerr and WK MacDonald, 'Cartography and the Undersea Arctic Region', *Journal of Navigation* Vol 37 No 2 1984.
AJ Kerr and MJ Keen, 'Hydrographic and Geologic Concerns of Implementing Article 76', *Int. Hydrographic Review* LXII (1) 1985.

AJ Kerr and WK MacDonald, 'Cartography of the Undersea Arctic Region', *Journal of Navigation*, Vol 37 No 2, 1984.

AJ Kerr and DF Dinn, 'The Use of Robots in Hydrography', *International Hydrographic Review*, January 1985.

AJ Kerr, 'Hydrography', *Canadian Encyclopaedia* Vol. II. Hurtig, Edmonton 1985. P.855

AJ Kerr, 'An Opinion – Computer Assistance – Does it increase Hydrographic Productivity', *Lighthouse Edition* 31 1985.c chart systems.

AJ Kerr, 'International Organisations and the Profession of Hydrography', *Commission 4 of the International Federation of Surveyors* XVII Congress 1986.

DC Kapoor and AJ Kerr, *A Guide to Maritime Boundary Delimitation*, Carswell Press 1986. 123 pages.

AJ Kerr, 'The Present Day Work of the International Hydrographic Organisation (IHO)', *Flash*, Quarterly Journal of Trinity House, September 1989.

AJ Kerr, 'Progress of ECDIS', keynote lecture at *Seminar on Electronic Chart Display Systems*, Tokyo 1989.

AJ Kerr, 'Development of Data Bases for ECDIS by the IHO and its Member States', *Motorship*, January 1991.

AJ Kerr, 'Status Report on Activities of IMO and IHO Concerning the Electronic Chart', *Int. Hydrographic Review* LXVII (2), July 1990.

AJ Kerr and Herman P Varma, 'Multi-Purpose Research Vessel Design in Canada', *Underwater Technology* Vol.12 No.2 1986.

AJ Kerr, 'Hydrography and the Digital Era', *Hydrographic Symposium*, Monaco May 1987.

AJ Kerr, K Manchester, R Reiniger and J Parsons, 'Designing a Multi-disciplinary Research Vessel. AJ Kerr, paper presented at *Oceans 87*, Halifax, NS

AJ Kerr, 'Pilot Books, Sailing Guides and Charts for Yachtsmen', *Journal of Institute of Navigation*, 1990.

AJ Kerr, 'Marine Positioning Requirements for Nautical Charts in the Twenty First Century', presented at *IMAP*, Miami 1990.

AJ Kerr, 'IHO Efforts in Developing Countries', *Int. Hydrographic*

Review, LXVI (1), January 1989.

AJ Kerr, 'A Worldwide Electronic Navigational Chart Database – an examination', *Navigation News*, June 1993

AJ Kerr, Geodetic Datums for Paper and Digital Charts of the Future. AJ Kerr .Seminar of East Asian Hydrographic Commission of the IHO. November 1993.

AJ Kerr, 'The Need for International Hydrographic Standards', paper presented at seminars in Kuala Lumpur and Jakarta arranged by Norwegian Trade Council. 1993.

AJ Kerr, 'ECDIS, Whose dealing with data?', *Navigation News*, March/April 1994.

AJ Kerr, 'Conceptual Model of a Regionally Integrated Data Base for ECDIS', *Int. Hydrographic Review* LXXI (2) 1994.

D Monahan, SB MacPhee and AJ Kerr, 'The Use of Natural Resource Maps in the management of Canadian Margins', *12th Conference of the Int. Cartographic Association*, Perth, Australia 1994.

AJ Kerr, 'A Worldwide Database for Digital Nautical Charts', *Journal of Institute of Navigation*, 1995.

AJ Kerr, *Continental Shelf Limits*, Oxford University Press 2000. 363 pages. Contributor on Historical Methods of Positioning at Sea.

AJ Kerr, 'Chapter 6 History of Cartography', *Cartography in the Twentieth Century*, University of Chicago, 2006. Includes: Marine chart; Marine Charting; Aerial imagery in hydrographic mapping and coastal charting; Marine charting by European nations.

#0061 - 260416 - C0 - 210/148/13 - PB - DID1435725